D1087441

KIERKEGAARD AND THE LIMITS OF
THE ETHICAL

KIERKEGAARD AND THE LIMITS OF THE ETHICAL

Anthony Rudd

CLARENDON PRESS · OXFORD
1993

Oxford University Press, Walton Street, Oxford OX2 6DP
Oxford New York Toronto
Delhi Bombay Calcutta Madras Karachi
Kuala Lumpur Singapore Hong Kong Tokyo
Nairobi Dar es Salaam Cape Town
Melbourne Auckland Madrid
and associated companies in
Berlin Ibadan

Oxford is a trade mark of Oxford University Press

Published in the United States
by Oxford University Press Inc., New York

British Library Cataloguing in Publication Data
Data available

Library of Congress Cataloging in Publication Data
Rudd, Anthony.
Kierkegaard and the limits of the ethical/Anthony Rudd.
p. cm.
1. Kierkegaard, Søren, 1813–1855—Ethics. 2. Religion and ethics.
3. Self (Philosophy) I. Title.
B4378.E8R83 1993 198'.9—dc20 92–42260
ISBN 0–19–824024–4

1 3 5 7 9 10 8 6 4 2

Typeset by Cambrian Typesetters
Frimley, Surrey
Printed in Great Britain by
Bookcraft (Bath) Ltd., Midsomer Norton, Avon.

To my Parents

PREFACE

THIS book is an attempt to say something about the nature of ethics and religion, about their problematic status in the modern world, and about the possible justifications for ethical and religious commitment. It is also a discussion of, and an attempt to evaluate, some of the main ideas of Søren Kierkegaard. It is both of these things at once because I have found Kierkegaard's ideas on ethics and religion profoundly illuminating. This is therefore my attempt to follow—though not uncritically—Kierkegaard's thinking as a guide to these problems.

Jim Hankinson remarks that 'Anglo-Saxon analytic philosophers are inclined to despise Existentialism for not being sufficiently analytic: Existentialists are inclined to despise Anglo-Saxon analytic philosophers for simply not being sufficiently.'[1] My own philosophical training was in the mainstream 'Anglo-Saxon analytic' philosophy referred to. And, certainly, Kierkegaard—or 'existentialism', or 'Continental philosophy'—were not usually referred to much by philosophers of this persuasion. One aim of this book is to show analytical philosophers that Kierkegaard is relevant to their concerns, and offers a fertile source of ideas which can be applied to contemporary debates. I hope it will also be of interest to students of Kierkegaard to see, rather than another work of historical scholarship, an attempt to make philosophical use of his ideas. And, thirdly, I hope that it may be of use to anyone—whether or not acquainted with either Kierkegaard or modern analytic philosophy—who is concerned about the nature of morality and/or religion, and about why—if at all—we should be either moral or religious.

The bulk of the work for this book was done at Lincoln College, Oxford, between 1986 and 1988, and was presented as an M.Litt. thesis there (Chapter 2, though, is entirely new, and Chapter 4 in particular has been substantially revised). I would like to thank my supervisors there—Dr Michael Ayers, Patrick

---

[1] J. Hankinson, *The Bluffer's Guide to Philosophy* (Morsham, 1985), 49.

Gardiner, Revd Oliver O'Donovan, and Gabrielle Taylor—for their helpful comments on my various drafts. Hubert Eiholzer not only typed the final version of the book, but also offered valuable criticisms of what he was typing; my particular thanks are due to him and to Amy. I am also grateful to other friends for encouragement—especially Per and Janet Ahlberg, Roderick Millar, and Barth Landor.

A.R.

CONTENTS

BIOGRAPHICAL NOTE

This is not a historical or biographical study of Kierkegaard, but a brief note on the man and his writings may be helpful to some readers.

Søren Aabye Kierkegaard was born in 1813 in Copenhagen. His father, a wealthy self-made businessman, encouraged his obvious intellectual and imaginative abilities, but also imposed a peculiarly harsh and gloomy religious upbringing on him. At Copenhagen University Kierkegaard—nominally a student of theology—enjoyed a relaxed and mildly bohemian lifestyle, while pursuing his own literary and philosophical interests. A sense of inner emptiness and futility—attested to in the journal that he started to keep at this time and maintained for the rest of his life—led him back to a more serious ethico-religious attitude. Reconciled to his father shortly before the latter's death in 1838, he completed his theological studies and became engaged to a young girl, Regine Olsen.

On the verge of settling down to a conventional life as a married man with a respectable clerical or academic career, Kierkegaard broke away. The exact motives for his decision not to marry Regine remain obscure, but the decision was certainly extremely painful for him. Following the break, he devoted himself to writing, while living off the wealth inherited from his father. His major early works were ascribed to pseudonyms—sometimes several pseudonyms within a single book—for complex reasons which I discuss briefly in Chapter 1.2. *Either/Or* appeared in 1843, rapidly followed by *Fear and Trembling* and *Repetition*; *The Concept of Anxiety* and *Philosophical Fragments* were published in 1844; *Stages on Life's Way* in 1845; and his *magnum opus*, the ironically named *Concluding Unscientific Postscript*, in 1846. *Two Ages*, a long book review in which Kierkegaard digressed to give his most sustained commentary on social and political matters, appeared shortly afterwards.

These works—philosophical, psychological, literary, literary-critical—had all circled round the question of religion without being definitely religious. Kierkegaard had also published some more explicitly religious discourses under his own name. From 1847 onwards these became his main form of literary expression. The stylistic and intellectual brilliance of his writing was unaffected, but the ironic indirectitudes of the earlier works gave way to a stern and direct presentation of Christian teaching. *Edifying Discourses in Various Spirits* (which includes the long discourse *Purity of Heart is to Will One Thing*) and *Works of Love* appeared in 1847, and *Christian Discourses* in 1848. *The Sickness unto Death*—which reverted to a more philosophical style—and the sharply polemical *Training in Christianity* were both written in 1848 but not published until 1849 and 1850 respectively. After 1850 Kierkegaard published little, but his journals record the increasing contempt that he was coming to feel for the established (Lutheran) Church of Denmark. In 1854 he began a journalistic and pamphleteering campaign against the Church, which he accused of hypocrisy and of betraying the Christian message. During 1855, in the midst of the controversy he had stirred up, Kierkegaard collapsed in the street; he died a few weeks later from a disease that was never clearly diagnosed.

LIST OF ABBREVIATIONS

The following abbreviations have been used for Kierkegaard's works, full details of which will be found in the Bibliography

CA	*The Concept of Anxiety*
ChD	*Christian Discourses*
CUP	*Concluding Unscientific Postscript*
Dru	*The Journals of Søren Kierkegaard*
E/O	*Either/Or*
FT	*Fear and Trembling*
JC	*Johannes Climacus, or, De omnibus dubitandum est*
Journals	*Søren Kierkegaard's Journals and Papers*
LB	*The Lilies of the Field and the Birds of the Air*
LY	*The Last Years: Journals, 1853–55*
PhF	*Philosophical Fragments*
P of H	*Purity of Heart is to Will One Thing*
SLW	*Stages on Life's Way*
SUD	*The Sickness unto Death*
TA	*Two Ages: A Literary Review*
TC	*Training in Christianity*
W of L	*Works of Love*

Please note that all biblical quotations are from the Authorized Version, and that, throughout this book, when I refer to any individual in the abstract, and write 'he', 'his', etc., this is to be understood as shorthand for 'he or she', 'his or her', etc. I adopt this convention for stylistic convenience, but it is worth noting that it has been defended on specifically feminist grounds by Sabina Lovibond (*Realism and Imagination in Ethics* (Oxford,

1983), 4): '[T]he "abstract individual" of philosophical literature is after all a male individual with a distinctive masculine set of problems and concerns, and it seems preferable at the moment to maintain an explicit awareness of this fact, rather than try to gloss it over with futile reformist turns of phrase.'

1

DISENGAGEMENT

1.1. THE DISENGAGED VIEW

Central to the argument of this book is the claim that the status of ethics in the modern world has been rendered deeply problematical by the rise of what I shall call the 'Disengaged View'. What do I mean by this term? It is the outlook that is obtained at the end of a process of self-transcendence, of abstraction from what is particular and peculiar about one's own standpoint. In fact, there is probably no final end-point to this process; rather, what we have are a series of perspectives which approximate with increasing closeness to the ideal of total disengagement. Describing this process, Thomas Nagel writes of

a polarity. At one end is the point of view of a particular individual, having a specific constitution, situation and relation to the rest of the world. From here the direction of movement towards greater objectivity involves, first, abstraction from the individual's specific spatial, temporal and personal position in the world, then from the features that distinguish him from other humans, then gradually from the forms of perception and action characteristic of humans, and away from the narrow range of a human scale in space, time and quantity, towards a conception of the world which, as far as possible, is not the view from anywhere within it. There is probably no end-point to this process, but its aim is to regard the world as centreless, with the viewer as just one of its contents.[1]

I agree with Nagel that the tension between the ideal of disengagement and the fact that we are, nevertheless, small, finite, limited creatures gives rise to a host of philosophical (and other) problems. I want to consider what happens when an individual disengages himself from the ethical outlook and

---

[1] T. Nagel, 'Subjective and Objective', in his *Mortal Questions* (Cambridge, 1981), 206.

customs of the particular community into which he is born, in order to rise to a more objective view of such matters. To set the scene for this discussion, and to clarify further what I mean by disengagement and what I think its significance for ethics is—and also to provide a broad historical context for my account of Kierkegaard's thought—I have thought it most helpful to set out an impressionistic sketch of certain aspects of intellectual (and social) history. Obviously, to cover adequately the ground over which I shall skim in the next few pages would take a substantial volume; what follows is merely a sketch.

Consider first a closed, 'primitive' society; or the sort of society depicted by Homer. In this kind of society individuals identify with their social roles. A child is born into a clan, a caste. He is brought up to think of himself not as an individual who happens to have been born into a certain position in a particular society, but simply as a member of that society, occupying a certain position within it. The duties and rights that go with that position are fairly clear and unambiguous; certain standards of behaviour and the objective criteria by which anyone is judged to have performed badly or well in the tasks that are incumbent upon him, go with the social roles that define the identities of members of such societies. And the virtues or excellences that enable anyone to perform his or her role—as king, as wife, as bard—are also clearly defined. 'Morality and social structure are in fact one and the same in heroic society. There is only one set of social bonds. Morality as something distinct does not yet exist. Evaluative questions are questions of social fact.'[2] To be good is to perform one's social role successfully, and there are criteria to establish definitely how well one has performed.

Such societies are uncritical, in that their members identify themselves with their roles; the social order, and their part in it, is seen as being as objective as the natural order. And correct behaviour is simply behaviour that is in accordance with the customs, norms, taboos of society. No different set of standards is even contemplated. Into this uncritical society may now come disruptive forces—economic changes dissolving rigid class barriers, contacts with different cultures, and so on. And in

[2] A. MacIntyre, *After Virtue: A Study in Moral Theory* (London, 1981), 116.

these circumstances the process of disengagement begins. People begin to see that the social order is mutable, and that there are alternative ways of organizing a human society. And, in realizing this, they start to become aware of themselves as individuals; they cease to see the social roles that they play as wholly defining their identities. It is in such circumstances that moral philosophy is born—some people start to question social customs, to ask why they should accept the familiar constraints on their behaviour. Certain reflective individuals start to ask: 'What is the right way for a human being to live? What is the good life for man?' To ask such general questions is to stand back from one's society and one's own place in it, and attempt to find a more universal criterion. Regarding myself simply as a human being, I ask: 'What is the appropriate, satisfying, happy life for a human being?' And the answer may tell me that it cannot be lived in my society. Hence the execution of Socrates— to ask the question, to appeal to standards more universal, 'higher', than those of society and tradition, is itself a dissolution of the social bond, no matter what answers were or were not returned.

With the decline of the Greek *polis*, and the emergence of great empires to which their subjects could feel no organic relation, disengagement and individualism became social fact. All of Greek ethics is a search for a conception of the 'good life for man', that is, for *eudaimonia*, a fully satisfying way of life. The presupposition of this ethical quest is that there is such a thing as a fixed human nature; we can stand back from the political societies in which we happen to have been born, but we cannot stand back from our own essence. In this context, a 'fact–value distinction' cannot even arise—one's idea of what the good life is for man depends on what one thinks a man is.

One can distinguish two main types of ethical anthropology in Greek thought (though Aristotle, the greatest Greek moral philosopher, tends to hover between them and cannot be simply enlisted in either camp). These could be called the empirical and the metaphysical. The former type of theory simply asks what, as a matter of fact, does make people happy. Epicurus replies, a life of moderate pleasures, prudent self-concern, and avoidance of pain, carried on in retreat from political society. Callicles replies, a life of political power and honour, combined with a vigorous pursuit of pleasure and the satisfaction of one's appetites. The trouble with this sort of theory is, of course, that all sorts of things make people happy, give them satisfaction, even lasting satisfaction. To expect a single answer to the question 'What is the good life' from a purely empirical study of human nature and of human tastes looks rather optimistic.

The second approach, which I labelled 'metaphysical', puts its anthropology within the context of a cosmology, to use the word in its etymological sense; an account of the world as a cosmos, a universal order, in which man has a definite place. This type of theory involves a kind of re-engagement; standing back from my position in the order of political society, which may not adequately or fully define my identity, I find it defined by my place in the order of the cosmos as a whole. Again, the standards governing my behaviour are set by my position within a wider order, because it is that position that defines my essential nature. Plato's ethics derives from his view that what a human being essentially is, is a reasoner. By virtue of my reason, I participate in a higher realm, that of incorporeal essences. And it is there that I really belong; this physical life is an exile from my true home.

So long as we have the body accompanying our reason in its enquiries, so long as our souls are befouled by this evil admixture, we shall assuredly never possess that which we desire, to wit, truth . . . If we are to have clear knowledge of anything, we must get rid of the body and let the soul by itself behold objects by themselves.[3]

Aristotle retains enough of this view to declare that the life of pure intellectual contemplation is the highest and happiest that there is. In Stoicism we have the ideal of living according to nature or reason—interchangeable concepts, since, for the Stoics, the nature of which we are a part is a manifestation or embodiment of divine *logos*.

What I have called the 'metaphysical' approach to ethical anthropology also prevails in the great religions. Again, what is found in their moral teaching is an account of the essential features of human nature, and, derived from that, an account of the appropriate behaviour and way of life. In Christianity my

[3] Plato, *Phaedo*, trans. R. Hackforth (Cambridge, 1972), 66 b, d–e.

essential nature is defined by my relationship to God. As His creature, made in His image, I can find fulfilment only by living in the knowledge and love of God—which finds expression in a universal love (*agape*) for my fellow men. But, alienated from this life by sin, I have to struggle constantly against the warp in my own nature pulling me towards self-destruction. Christian ethics is a prescription of behaviour that is appropriate to this situation. If Christianity is true, then my problematic relationship to God is what must be central to my moral life. The virtues that derive from that relationship take precedence over those that arise from my social position. In Augustine's classic formulation, the Christian is essentially a citizen of the City of God—and the duties that arise from this role take precedence over those arising from his membership of any earthly city. (Later writers were unfortunately less guarded than Augustine in identifying the City of God with an all too human Church.)

For Judaism and its Christian and Islamic offshoots, an absolute standard is provided by revelation, against which the morality of existing societies can be judged. The individual appeals from the law of his society to the law of God. But a limit to this disengagement is set by the fundamental belief in this world as a divine creation, however infested with sin; and the hope remains of the eventual establishment of the Messianic kingdom or the Islamic state, where the law of God becomes the law of society, and hence the disengagement forced upon the righteous individual by the wickedness of his society ceases to be necessary. A far more rigorous ideal of disengagement is found in Buddhism and Hinduism, and—expressed with the greatest clarity and rigour—in the Gnostic sects and the Manichaean religion. The prophet Mani preached the evil of the physical world, and identified the person with the soul—a fragment from the higher world of light, trapped in the darkness of a material universe created by demons to imprison it. In this situation, my aim can only be to escape from this miserable exile in an alien world, and return to the higher realm to which I truly belong. This requires the most drastic disengagement. My body and its needs and appetites are not really mine, in that they do not express my true nature. Rather, they are my fetters. And so too are the whole set of social obligations and duties, the whole of 'worldly' morality. Either I passively opt out of society to concentrate on the liberation of my soul; or—as was recommended by some Gnostic sects, such as the Carpocratians and the followers of Simon Magus—I should actively defy a morality that taught successful living in an evil world, by deliberately embracing criminality and vice as spiritual disciplines. This sense that the world is alien and incorrigibly wicked, and that the only path the wise man can take is one of flight from it, takes us to an extreme point of disengagement.

> From the day when my heart came to love the Truth,
> I no longer have trust in anything in the world.
> In mother and father . . .
> In brothers and sisters . . .
> In what is made and created,
> In the whole world and its works;
> I have no trust in the world.
> After my soul alone I go searching about,
> Which to me is worth generations and worlds.
> I went and found my soul—
> What to me are all the worlds? . . .
> I went and found truth,
> As she stands at the outer rim of the worlds.[4]

Yet even Manichaeanism derives its ethics from an account of the essential nature of man, and his place in the cosmos. In the higher world of light I am at home, I have a place in the order to which I truly belong. I disengage myself from this dark world in order to return to the harmonious cosmos of which I am really a part. It is only in the last few centuries[5] that the full notion of disengagement has developed; one in which the individual separates himself from this order without the hope of finding a higher or better one in which he can take his part. The most influential form that this radical ideal has taken has been scientific.

Modern natural science, as it has developed since the seventeenth century, is an attempt to see the world objectively. The ideal scientist abstracts from all that is merely personal about his outlook; he abstracts, too, from the prejudices and

---

[4] A Mandean hymn, quoted in H. Jonas, *The Gnostic Religion* (Boston, 1963), 90–1.

[5] In a fuller treatment of these issues, I would have to qualify this claim by saying something about classical scepticism.

customs of his culture. Furthermore, he abstracts from those forms of perception and thought that are specifically human (hence the denial of the objective reality of secondary qualities). His aim is to become—*qua* scientist—a pure rational knower, understanding the world by using a scientific method that is sheerly rational, which will be used by any rational being, however unlike a human being it may be, so long as its reason remains unclouded by prejudice, superstition, and so on. And he aspires to see the world from no place within it, to enjoy what Nagel calls the 'view from nowhere'. Indexicals are dispensed with; all places and all times are spread out before the scientist's dispassionate gaze.

At the same time, the scientist remains a little animal, confined to the surface of one not especially significant planet for a life-span of a few decades. And his ambition to step back from himself and from his own species leads him to try and understand human beings on the same principles as any other natural phenomenon. *Qua* subject of science, I am the pure, detached, rational knower; *qua* object of science, I am a complicated piece of physical machinery, in principle no different from any other. How are these two perceptions to be held together? It is hardly surprising that at the beginning of the scientific revolution Descartes should have revived Platonic dualism. The conscious soul is a substance quite distinct from the body-machine. Today, those philosophers who make most of the natural sciences tend to be materialists, believing 'that we can give a complete account of man in purely physico-chemical terms'.[6] But behind this monism still lurks a concealed dualism. We are told that we should look to science rather than to art, religion, etc., for the 'complete' account of man, because it is in science alone that we strip away all that is merely subjective, and, rising to an absolute point of view, come to see the world as it really is. Only by a rigorous process of intellectual asceticism and self-transcendence—which demands all our 'spiritual' powers of rationality, disengagement, self-consciousness—can we come to see that we are just bits of physical machinery, and that talk of spirits and souls is mere illusion.

---

[6] D. M. Armstrong, 'The Nature of Mind', in C. V. Borst (ed.), *The Mind/Brain Identity Theory* (London, 1970), 67.

There is something very odd about this view, and I think that radical materialism does manage to saw off the branch on which it sits, when it claims that all truths about the world can be expressed in the language of physics. For amongst the terms that cannot be translated into that language are 'rationality', 'truth', 'probability', 'explanatory power', 'meaning', 'reference' (despite Hartry Fields' attempt to argue the contrary!), and these are necessary for physicists (or anyone else) to understand what they are doing. It would take me too far afield to develop this argument fully;[7] I merely want to suggest that the spiritual ideal of disengagement and self-transcendence is alive and well in contemporary scientistic philosophy. Charles Taylor has even suggested that the appeal of this type of philosophy derives mainly from the ideal; that this is what attracts people to radical reductionist theories that are intellectually not at all plausible. 'Supporting the impetus to naturalism . . . stands an attachment to a certain picture of the agent . . . it shows us as capable of achieving a certain kind of detachment from our world by objectifying it.'[8]

Of course, the vision of science as the work of the free, pure, disengaged reason has not gone unchallenged. There are those who claim that science is just Western, or male, or bourgeois ideology. More soberly, it has been pointed out by Kuhn and his successors that science is a co-operative human activity; the scientist is not a free-floating intelligence, but someone who at a particular time is initiated into an intellectual tradition and a community which does not invariably reach consensus by pure rational means. Lakatos and Feyerabend have thrown doubt on the idea that there is any one scientific method, distinguished by its rationality, which guarantees scientific success. Again, these are large debates into which I cannot get drawn here; my interest is in the wider cultural impact of the disengaged ideal as expressed in modern science, however much it may be an idealization of actual scientific practice.

Modern science was born around the same time as the

---

[7] But see H. Putnam, *Reason, Truth and History* (Cambridge, 1981), ch. 2; and id., 'Why There Isn't a Ready-Made World', and 'Why Reason Can't Be Naturalized', in *Realism and Reason* (Philosophical Papers, 3; Cambridge, 1983), *passim*.

[8] C. Taylor, 'Introduction', in *Human Agency and Language* (Philosophical Papers, 1; Cambridge, 1985), 4.

capitalist industrial-commercial society (the birth of the latter was rather more prolonged), and one does not have to be a Marxist to see this as something more than a coincidence. The ideal of disengagement is central to modern culture; it receives its most powerful intellectual expression in science (or in idealized accounts of science), but it is practically embodied in the individualism of our social life, as well as of our social thought. The idea of society as an organism is swept away and replaced by the idea of society as the result of a contractual agreement between autonomous individuals. Conservatives rightly criticized this account for its unreality, but this criticism remains rather ineffectual, for the myth of the social contract does reflect the social realities of an individualistic, capitalist society, in which 'all fixed, fast-frozen relations with their train of ancient and venerable prejudices and opinions are swept away'.[9]

Traditional ethics, as I argued above, was a mixture of social and religious duties. The two had become interwoven, the religious element always providing material for a potential criticism of the social, but usually finding a *modus vivendi* with it, and often lending an air of absolute authority to social rules and prohibitions. The Enlightenment rejected religion, or else reduced God to the level of a polite deistic gentleman whose irrelevance to morals was argued by familiar sophisms. As for society, my social role could no longer be thought of as defining what I essentially am; not because that is defined by some wider relationship, but because I am an autonomous individual; no relationship can define my identity—all remain external to what I essentially am.[10]

This is the radical idea of autonomy—that I can remain myself even after stepping back from all my relationships and roles.[11]

[9] K. Marx and F. Engels, 'Manifesto of the Communist Party', trans. S. Moore, in E. Kamenka (ed.), *The Portable Karl Marx* (Harmondsworth, 1983), 207.

[10] It is not fanciful to see the insistence on the externality of relations by empiricist philosophy as connected to this social development, especially if we contrast both the logic and the social philosophy of empiricism with those of Hegel and Bradley, who did believe—in both spheres—that an individual is defined by its relations, and therefore that individuality is relative.

[11] Even—if I still believe in Him—from my relationship to God. This is what the argument that it is only right to obey God's commands if we have independent reason to think them good amounts to; my relationship to God does not define my identity, tell me what, essentially, I am, as for a Christian it must.

This creates problems for ethics. For if all my relationships and roles are contingent to me, how can absolute standards of correct behaviour be derived from them? What can be called the characteristic ethic of the Enlightenment was a fairly simple hedonism and utilitarianism. This can still be regarded as an attempt to derive an account of the good life for man from an account of what a man essentially is; but that account is a radically simplified—not to say simplistic—one. A human being is an individual piece of psycho-physical machinery. The happy life for such a being is one in which pleasure, thought of as a sensation, is maximized, and pain minimized. How this outlook was supposed to generate a social morality was another question, and moral philosophers had to embark on the awkward task of finding reasons to convince a hard-boiled character, who accepted that he was indeed simply an individual pleasure-consumer, that he should be concerned to give pleasure to others. But, assuming that this problem could be solved, or at least swept under the carpet, morality became a matter of calculation. How could society be so ordered as to maximize the amount of pleasure felt within it? As has been pointed out by some of its critics (notably Williams), utilitarianism demands a drastic disengagement. As a moral agent, I must aspire to the 'view from nowhere'; survey the social world without taking into account my place within it, and approve of policies that will maximize the general good, whatever their effect on me. As in scientific materialism, a chasm opens up between myself as subject and myself as object. In the former role I am a disengaged, impartial calculator; in the latter, a piece of pleasure-consuming machinery. And one might well ask how it maximizes the pleasure of the latter (and thus becomes rational for him) to play the part of the former.

One further step towards the disengaged ideal still remained to be taken, and it was taken, at the end of the eighteenth century, by Kant. Kant's epistemology can be seen as challenging the ideal, for it was a denial of the possibility of absolute knowledge. From the beginnings of philosophy it had been believed that one was rewarded for the arduous process of disengagement by coming to see things as they really are—one is taken beyond appearance to reality. This Kant denied. What we can know can never be more than appearance, however strenuously we seek to purify our intellects. We are unable to see things absolutely, in themselves. The notion of the thing in itself, often derided and rejected by Kant's successors, is vital to his philosophy, and saves it from collapsing into a mere variant of the positivism or empiricism according to which the being of things is exhausted by their appearance. On that view, we can have absolute and exhaustive knowledge of how things really are; it is this that Kant denies, and this denial that gives his work its significance as an epistemology of finitude.

But Kant is concerned to combat scepticism; he wants to provide guarantees for the security of our scientific knowledge. The fundamental concepts that science employs—cause, substance, even time and space—are not justified because they correspond to the basic structural features of reality, but because they form the necessary framework for our thinking. The old metaphysical supports for our 'conceptual scheme' have been removed, but shiny new transcendental ones have taken their place. And these are the same for all thinking individuals.[12] Hence Kant's epistemology remains extemely abstract; it is concerned with the conditions of knowledge for a knowing subject in general.

The same pattern is found in his ethics. He sets out to discover the conditions of rationality in action; these are to hold good for any rational agent. Again, morality, like science, is not guaranteed or supported by anything external; not by Platonic forms, not by Aristotelian ideas about the *ergon* or function of man, not by utilitarian concern with natural desires for pleasure, and not by God. Morality is just rationality in action—it is the condition of rational consistency in action, and, as such, it is entirely autonomous and self-supporting. But this conception of ethics is the most radically disengaged one that has ever been conceived. To act morally, I must abstract from my social relationships and roles, from my relationship with God (if I believe in Him), and from my very humanity. I must regard myself simply as a pure, rational agent. In this, Kant goes much further than previous Enlightenment thinkers. They too had urged us to think of ourselves as autonomous rational agents, but, for them, the free agent was still essentially a human being,

[12] Though Kant does consider the possibility of beings who would not order their precepts according to the forms of intuition—space and time.

a member of a particular biological species, with all its natural desires and needs. It is from this standpoint that we must decide how to live and act.[13] But, for Kant, in order to be moral, I must disengage from my humanity.

Put like this, Kant's ethic sounds Manichaean. But in one sense it is less drastic than that, though in another sense it is more so. It is less drastic, in that Kant does not simply repudiate worldly and physical desires; what he does insist is that the courses of action they demand be approved by the tribunal of practical reason. Before I can act, I must ask myself: Is this action acceptable as that of a rational being? And the idea is that this constraint on agency will produce a set of maxims that we can recognize as those of traditional morality. Kant was not a moral reformer or innovator. He starts, in the *Grundlegung*, from an analysis of the 'common rational knowledge of morality'—in other words, the 'language of morals' as spoken around Königsberg, c.1780—and he is concerned to show that—and how—this 'knowledge' is well founded. As, in the first *Critique*, he had tried to show that—and how—Newtonian mechanics was well founded.

Kant's ethics represent a more drastic demand for disengagement than Manichaeanism, in that the good Manichee was not attempting to live autonomously, but to act in loyalty to the higher world in which he really belonged. But Kant insists that morality is total autonomy. What I am essentially has been stripped down to the bare minimum. I am a rational agent, and should therefore act rationally. My standards of behaviour cannot be set by anything external to this bare rationality—not by society, not by God, not by my own human nature and its 'pathological' desires. They are set simply by the demand for rational consistency in action. (Admittedly, Kant spoils this rigorous picture a bit by arguing that in moral action I gain a sort of access to the noumenal realm, where I may hope to discover God, freedom, and immortality. But this is a consequence of morality and not a basis for it.)

Kantian ethics has a pivotal significance in the story I am sketching here. For, according to Kant, a substantive, universal, and objectively true morality can be worked out from the

---

[13] Cf. in this connection the Enlightenment's enthusiasm for nature and for 'natural' standards of behaviour, as opposed to merely social or religious ones.

disengaged perspective. Abstracting from all richer accounts of human nature, and regarding a human being in isolation from his or her social roles or relationships, simply as a rational agent, we can derive a full systematic account of our rights and duties. In ethics, as in science, disengagement is the way to truth. Obviously, this conception is very attractive to modern liberalism; it promises to establish moral truths that hold good for people in all societies and circumstances, while making no appeal to contentious metaphysical or religious accounts of human nature. Kantian moral thought, however, has always had to struggle against the charge of vacuity, the suspicion that the description of a person as simply a rational agent is just too thin for any significant moral constraints to be derived from it. Many critics, starting with Hegel, have argued that Kant's criterion of universalizability fails to rule out any course of action at all. Of course, Kant has his defenders, and there are a number of contemporary philosophers—for instance, Nagel and Gewirth—who have attempted, with original and ingenious arguments, to revive the Kantian project of justifying morality by showing it to be a condition of rational action.[14] To provide an adequately detailed critique of Kantian and neo-Kantian ethics would take at least a book in itself; I have no space to provide it here. I can only refer to the familiar anti-Kantian arguments, and simply state that I do not believe that Kant himself, or any of his successors, have managed to show that any serious moral constraints can be derived from simply considering the conditions of rational agency. Nor do I think that this can be done. What follows rests on the premiss that the Kantian project is a failure.

If this premiss is accepted, then we are faced by a dilemma, which can be put very simply in the question: disengagement or morality? If, after acknowledging that no moral constraints follow from the bare, disengaged picture of a man as a pure rational agent, one still continues to accept that picture, then one is left with some form of ethical subjectivism. The ideal of autonomy, the refusal to derive morals from rich descriptions of human nature, the image of the pure, rational self standing back from its social relations and regarding them as contingencies:

[14] One should also mention the work of Habermas, who has attempted to derive an ethics from the norms governing interpersonal linguistic communications, which he attempts to formulate as a 'universal pragmatics'.

these are retained from Kant, but the moral rationalism is rejected. As a result, we are left with the familiar picture of the free agent choosing—or creating—his values for himself. Thus Hare tells us that each one of us is free to decide for himself what he will call good; for 'thin', general moral concepts, such as 'good' or 'right', there are no objective criteria of application, as there are with such 'thick' concepts as 'rudeness' or 'courage'. We are free to choose, in disengagement from our social norms, what we shall call good.[15] For Sartre, to act from unquestioning acceptance of some social role, to act as a waiter acts, or as a good citizen acts, is Bad Faith, the primal sin. There remains in Sartre—as in many subjectivists—a kind of vestigial moral objectivism. In his philosophy 'existence precedes essence'— man is nothing but a continual capacity for self-transcendence, for stepping back from the objects of his consciousness—even from his empirical personality. So, for Sartre, human dignity, nobility, lie in accepting our lack of substantiality, and refusing to run away from it by pretending that we have fixed essences. 'Man is nothing other than what he makes of himself . . . But what do we mean to say by this but that man is of greater dignity than a stone or a table?'[16]

Sartre's philosophy is probably the most striking embodiment of the vision of disengagement to be propounded in modern times. But, of course, a moral subjectivist does not need to take on board the entire Sartrean metaphysics. Subjectivism derives from the sense that there is no universal account of human nature rich enough for a substantive ethics to be derived from it. Bernard Williams remarks that considerations of human nature 'will radically underdetermine . . . the ethical options . . . I find it hard to believe that human beings could turn out to have a much more determinate nature than is suggested by what we already know, one that timelessly demanded a life of a particular kind.'[17] Williams's scepticism here is directed against recent attempts to revive an Aristotelian view of ethics. Neo-Aristotelian moral philosophers, such as Philippa Foot, have attempted to determine the virtues necessary for leading a full and satisfying human life. But in what does this consist? As

---

[15] Cf. R. M. Hare, *Freedom and Reason* (Oxford, 1963), ch. 2.
[16] J.-P. Sartre, *Existentialism and Humanism*, trans. P. Mairet (London, 1948), 28.
[17] B. Williams, *Ethics and the Limits of Philosophy* (London, 1985), 153.

Williams says, 'We . . . have the idea that there are many and various forms of human excellence which will not all fit together into a one harmonious whole, so any determinate ethical outlook is going to represent some kind of specialisation of human possibilities.'[18]

Of course, apart from traditional theological accounts which have insisted that there is one overriding form of human excellence, there have been other influential attempts to derive a single universal account of the good life for man from an essentialist account of human nature. One thinks especially of Marx's vision of social labour freed from alienation, and of Nietzsche's monistic psychology and ethics of the Will to Power.[19] Even apart from such ambitious projects, we may still find a measure of agreement on which things are good, and on the importance of certain virtues. But it seems unlikely that, confining ourselves to a 'naturalistic or, again, historical conception of human nature',[20] we will be able to derive from it a single determinate ethic that can be universally applied.

The Enlightenment's stress on disengagement provoked in time a reaction in the form of the Romantic movement, with its sense of man's unity with nature, and embeddedness in traditions, and its re-evaluations of the importance of emotional life. This had a substantial influence on post-Kantian philosophy, and especially on Hegel, whose whole philosophy can be seen as an attempt to synthesize Enlightenment and Romanticism, disengagement and rootedness in the world. Fundamental to Hegel's thought is the idea of a threefold pattern: an initial, unselfconscious immersion in a wider order; then a movement of disengagement, a breaking away from that order; and thirdly a reintegration into the order, but on a higher, self-conscious level, preserving what has been gained in the second movement. Hegel sees this pattern as the key to understanding the whole of reality, but he is most plausible, and has been most influential,

---

[18] Ibid.
[19] There is, of course, in Nietzsche a deep suspicion of monistic systematic thinking ('The Will to a System is a lack of integrity': F. Nietzsche, *Twilight of the Idols*, trans. R. J. Hollingdale, publ. with *The Antichrist* (Harmondsworth, 1982), 25). For all that, in his last years he was attempting to construct a system of his own, which would make the 'Will to Power' the key to explaining not only all of human behaviour, but the universe as a whole.
[20] Williams, *Ethics and the Limits of Philosophy*, 153.

in his account of human culture and history. For Hegel, one should not think simply in terms of a conflict between an immersion in social values and a radical individualism. Man is both social and individual; the process of disengagement was necessary for man to realize his individuality, but this individuality is empty and unsatisfying if it is realized simply in opposition to society. Hence the need for the final synthesis of individual and social values. Man finds his true fulfilment not in the abstractions of Kantian morality, but in conformity to the laws and customs of society—but a society that has learnt to understand the value of the individual.

Hegel's thought can be developed in various ways. It can form the basis for a conservative morality of social integration. Writing later in the nineteenth century, Bradley attacked the Kantian and utilitarian demands for disengagement in ethics, and pointed out that the free, self-conscious individual is himself a social product, and the product not of society in the abstract, but of a specific society. Bradley writes: 'The soul within him is saturated, is filled, is qualified by, it has assimilated, has got its substance, has built itself up from, it is one and the same life with the universal life, and if he turns against this, he turns against himself.'[21] There is certainly much that is right in this argument. It is only by having the norms, standards, and customs of a particular society imposed upon him; only by learning the language spoken in that community and being initiated into its traditions; only by being thus assimilated into some particular historical community and culture, that a child is transformed from a merely biological into a cultural being. Only in this way does he become an individual—with a mind of his own, and capable of rational thought and moral judgement.

Granted all this, what follows for morality? For Bradley, since man is a social animal, the good life for man is life lived in society. And not society in the abstract, but a specific historical community: the one in which he lives and which has, in large measure, given him his mind and his soul. Instead of making futile efforts to disengage from his social world, he should accept his 'station' within it; perform the duties that go with that

[21] F. H. Bradley, 'My Station and its Duties', in his *Ethical Studies*, 2nd edn. (Oxford, 1927), 172.

station, and enjoy the rights that it confers upon him. In this way he finds self-realization—the realization of himself not in futile opposition to his society, but as part of it; the realization of his true, namely his social, self.

Hegel's philosophy of history gives him the basis for a theory of overall progress, against which different societies can be judged and evaluated. If one retains Hegel's polemic against individualistic morality, but abandons his notion of historical progress, the resulting outlook becomes frankly relativistic. The good is for each individual to fit into his society, but there is no general criterion as to what is a good society. This point of view is an extremely conservative one, and, while this tradition of ethical thought certainly contains insights which need to be preserved, it will not do as a complete account of ethics. For a start it is simply inapplicable to a society as culturally fragmented as ours, and in which the ideal of disengagement is so powerful. When we are brought up to respect the ethical norms of our society, a large part of what we are taught is precisely respect for the ideals of autonomy and individualism. A Bradlean will say that liberalism is wrong; but the very existence of liberal individualism poses a problem for the advocates of an 'organic' society. If members of a society regard themselves as autonomous individuals, and do not identify themselves with their social roles, this in itself means that society is not functioning as an organism. There is an inevitable artificiality about attempts to return to a pre-individualistic society; we cannot just identify with our social roles—it is too late for that now. Once the ideal of the detached autonomous self has arisen, it is not possible simply to suppress it (short, perhaps, of a catastrophic war or revolution). And this means that it is always possible for me to step back from my 'station', and refuse to accept that an evaluation of me *qua* performer of some social role is an adequate evaluation of me as a person.[22]

So far I have sketched the development of the ideal of disengagement, which has taken us from the ethics of social

---

[22] In fairness to Bradley himself, it should be said that, good dialectician as he was, he never regarded the social morality propounded in 'My Station' as more than a half-truth. In the following chapter of *Ethical Studies* ('Ideal Morality', 223), we find him making such remarks as 'Man is not man at all, unless social, but man is not much above the beasts unless more than social.'

conformism, in which morality is derived from our identities as members of society; to religious ethics in which it is derived from our identity in relation to the cosmic set-up; to utilitarian hedonism, where it derives from our biological nature and desires; to Kantianism, where it derives simply from our identity as rational agents; and finally to subjectivism, in which it cannot be rationally grounded at all. It seems as though the process of disengagement is destructive of morality—though, as Nietzsche and others have noted, it is itself a moral ideal—because it undermines any attempt we might make to establish a stable and determinate identity. Does this mean that the idea of a universal and objective morality is an illusion? Or does it mean that the process of disengagement has been pushed too far? Many epistemologists and philosophers of science in this century have come to repudiate the notion of radical disengagement. Stuart Hampshire explicitly draws the parallel in opposing disengagement in both epistemology and ethics: 'I am arguing for the equivalent in ethics of a principle that has to be recognized in the theory of knowledge: that all perception of the external world is from a particular point of view, and the observer must take account of his particular standpoint.'[23]

In what follows, I want to explore these questions about the pressures that drive people either to adopt or to resist the disengaged view in ethical thinking and practice through a discussion of some of the main ideas of Kierkegaard. I want to show both that this makes a good framework for the understanding of Kierkegaard and that Kierkegaard's ideas can do much to clarify these problems.

1.2. THE RELEVANCE OF KIERKEGAARD

Borges once noted that 'every writer creates his own precursors. His work modifies our conception of the past, as it will modify the future.'[24] Since his death, Kierkegaard has suffered the fate of being hailed as a precursor of various intellectual and spiritual movements, most notably, perhaps, Sartrean existentialism.

[23] S. Hampshire, 'Introduction: From Nature to Second Nature', in his *Morality and Conflict* (Oxford, 1983), 9.
[24] J. L. Borges, 'Kafka and his Precursors', in *Labyrinths* (Harmondsworth, 1985), 236.

Accordingly, people have tended to read Sartre (and the Sartre of *Existentialism and Humanism* at that) back into Kierkegaard, and to condemn—or praise—the figure who emerges as a result for his irrationalism and extreme individualism. Of course, this picture of Kierkegaard is not entirely false; the Sartrean reading of his work is not just a misinterpretation. But it does represent a gross oversimplification of one of the most subtle and complex of modern writers. I want to suggest in this book that there is a great deal in Kierkegaard that is highly relevant to the problems discussed by contemporary Anglo-American moral philosophers, and that his writings constitute one of the best resources we have for coming to a better understanding of the problems created for ethics by the rise of the disengaged ideal.

I do not claim in my exegesis to be revealing the 'true' Kierkegaard. No doubt some of what I have to say will be one-sided, and in any case I discuss only a few of his many works in detail. I am certainly open to the accusation of 'creating' Kierkegaard as a precursor of certain contemporary philosophers, notably MacIntyre. But any interpretation is a dialogue between what has to be interpreted and the present concerns of the interpreter—which is why literary criticism, history—including the history of philosophy—and translations of classic works have to be done afresh by each new generation. This is not, of course, a defence of arbitrariness; I do not think I am reading into Kierkegaard what is not there, and I shall be quoting extensively from his works in support of my interpretations.

I have said that I have substantive philosophical ambitions as well as exegetical ones. I shall alternate between passages in which I follow Kierkegaard's texts closely, and those in which I explore the questions raised by those texts in my own way. I am concerned not only to report what Kierkegaard said, but also to bring out explicitly some lines of thought that seem to me to be implicit in his writings, to find arguments to support some of the conclusions that I find attractive but inadequately defended in his works, to develop more fully some ideas that he throws off in passing, and so on. In doing all this, I shall be drawing on the work of various contemporary philosophers, including Parfit, Williams, Foot, and—especially—MacIntyre, as well as on that of some of Kierkegaard's peers—Hegel, Schopenhauer, Nietzsche—using their ideas both to support my reconstruction of Kierkegaard and to contrast with it. The philosophical position that is reached at the end of this process is, I think, a very plausible one. In particular, it enables us to understand better both the strengths and the weaknesses of the currently fashionable neo-naturalistic movement in ethics, and also to understand better the relation of religion and ethics, and why—contrary to the view that many philosophers still seem to take for granted—someone's religious beliefs or disbeliefs should affect his or her ethical outlook.

No one who admires Kierkegaard and tries to write a systematic, rational reconstruction of his ideas can avoid a certain feeling of guilt. Kierkegaard was a deliberately unsystematic thinker; like other such thinkers—Nietzsche, the later Wittgenstein—he wrote 'for edification', not so that his fragments could be tidily arranged into a system. My excuse must be that to provide a synoptic overview of (part of) a writer's work is not necessarily the same as presenting it as an objective system. Kierkegaard liked to use a literary method of philosophizing, not just so as to communicate vividly certain doctrines that had initially been formulated in more abstract terms, but because to provide literary portraits of individuals is a more authentically existential way of philosophizing than writing formal treatises. In *Johannes Climacus* Kierkegaard argues that language, being inherently general, distorts reality in the act of grasping it, being unable to do justice to the particularity of things.[25] But literature can come closer to the particularity of existence than philosophy. Abstract concepts and doctrines remain useless and empty unless they can be applied to specific, concrete situations; thus Kierkegaard can make his ideas about the aesthetic life, for instance, come across to us by showing us what it means in concrete terms, by bringing aesthetes before the eye of the imagination in 'The Seducer's Diary', *Repetition*, 'In Vino Veritas'.

I cannot do justice to Kierkegaard's literary method in what follows; there is plenty of scope for literary-critical discussions of Kierkegaard, as well as philosophical ones. Better still would be discussions that combined literary with philosophical analyses, instead of making distinctions which are artificial in the best of

[25] Cf. *JC* 168.

cases, and especially so with regard to Kierkegaard.[26] However, I do not pretend to provide anything of the sort here; what follows is just philosophy. But, in any case, virtually any statement about a writer as multifaceted as Kierkegaard will need to be qualified; what I have said about his literary method certainly holds true for some of his books, but not for all of them. In *The Concept of Anxiety* and *The Sickness unto Death*, and also in parts of *Concluding Unscientific Postscript* and *Philosophical Fragments*, he cheerfully throws off sweeping generalizations and employs language of vertiginous abstraction.

I should perhaps say a word about my attitude to the question of Kierkegaard's pseudonyms. At one extreme, some commentators virtually ignore the fact that Kierkegaard published most of his major works under a variety of pseudonyms. At the other extreme are those who hold that none of the views expressed in the pseudonymous works can safely be attributed to Kierkegaard at all. I think one needs to distinguish between the different pseudonyms, which were employed for different purposes.

First, Kierkegaard uses pseudonyms to express views and attitudes with which he does not agree, but which he thinks need to be clearly and vividly expressed. This is the case with the various characters—'A', Johannes the Seducer, Constantin Constantius—who represent the aesthetic point of view. But even here Kierkegaard would agree with much of what they say—their psychological observations, their comments on art and culture. He presents his aesthetes as highly intelligent and perceptive men, who see things clearly and accurately—within the limits of their overall outlook.

The same is true of Judge William, Kierkegaard's ethical spokesman, into whose mouth Kierkegaard puts the best arguments for the ethical that he can think of. And he certainly saw those arguments as being valid—up to a point. The problem with the ethical is not that it is simply mistaken, but that it does not go far enough. Judge William's arguments are valid as against the aesthetes, but there are a whole series of other factors and problems with which the Judge does not really deal. Kierkegaard's whole account of the 'stages of life' rests on the

---

[26] Cf. L. Mackey, *Kierkegaard: A Kind of Poet* (Philadelphia, 1971), for an integrated literary/philosophical treatment.

belief that the progress from error to truth is best understood as a movement through progressively more adequate stages of partial truth. Each new stage is an advance on what went before, but is still inadequate from the perspective of the stages ahead. (In this, Kierkegaard is certainly a Hegelian; the difference is that, for Kierkegaard, the stages are to be lived through, not just contemplated dispassionately.) Accordingly, the pseudonyms who represent the different stages represent different levels of partial truth—Kierkegaard neither identifies with them wholly nor wholly repudiates them. One could in fact say the same of some of the works published in Kierkegaard's own name, which are religious in a generalized rather than a specifically Christian sense (what he called 'Religiousness A'). These (for example, *Purity of Heart*) do not represent the final truth, but an outlook that represents the highest purely human achievement prior to revelation.

Secondly, there are the pseudonyms that Kierkegaard uses for his more theoretical, less 'literary' works. These do not seem to me to indicate that Kierkegaard has any disagreement with the content of these works. The *Fragments* and *Postscript* were ascribed to Johannes Climacus, who differs from Kierkegaard himself in disclaiming any settled religious convictions of his own. This is appropriate, since these works are intended to perform a task of conceptual clarification which will aid clear thinking about religious issues; to this end, Kierkegaard wanted to write in a neutral way, to make it clear that his understanding of the nature of faith did not itself presuppose any religious commitment. Later, Kierkegaard used the pseudonym of Anti-Climacus for two of his most rigorously Christian works, *Training in Christianity* and *The Sickness unto Death*. This was because he felt that he did not succeed in living up to the stringent demands of those books, and therefore could not present them to the public directly, under his own name. One further factor in Kierkegaard's use of pseudonyms that should not be neglected is his simple enjoyment of the game, of appearing in different masks. It is hard to find a deeper reason than this for his ascription of *The Concept of Anxiety* to a pseudonym.

To summarize: we can take the more theoretical pseudonymous works roughly at face value; the more literary pseudonyms need to be treated rather differently, as voices in a developing argument that need to be contrasted with one another.

1.3. KIERKEGAARD'S THOUGHT: AN INTRODUCTORY OUTLINE

Before embarking on a detailed discussion of Kierkegaard's thought, it may be helpful to give a brief overview of its main contours. Towards the end of 1.1, I mentioned Hegel's concern to find a synthesis in which our rootedness and our capacity for disengagement could be reconciled, and full justice done to both. In the years following Hegel's death, his two most important critics—Marx and Kierkegaard—both accepted that this was the essential problem, but held that Hegel's solution was a purely abstract one, which failed to connect with reality. For Marx, the synthesis would only become real when a proletarian revolution ushered in a new society where 'the free development of each is the condition for the free development of all'.[27] Kierkegaard's departure from Hegel was more radical. For him, the synthesis is to be brought about not on the level of world history, through the transformation of society, but as a task for each individual to achieve for himself, within himself.

Kierkegaard describes the self as a self-conscious synthesis of 'the infinite and the finite, and the temporal and the eternal, of freedom and necessity'.[28] In each of these three sets of contrasting qualities, there is one that stands for our limitations, our 'rootedness', as I have called it, and one that stands for our power to transcend those limits, our capacity for 'disengagement'. Essentially, then, man is a synthesis of those two elements, but his nature is not simply given to him as settled and finished. As Kierkegaard rather bemusingly puts it: 'the self is not the relation but is the relation's relating itself to itself.'[29] In other words, a human being is not simply a combination of factors— as a chemical compound is—but is self-conscious; the synthesis of the different factors in a human being is the task of that human being, which he must actively strive for. The possibility therefore exists that the synthesis will not be properly developed and maintained, and that the elements in human nature will

---

[27] Marx and Engels, 'Manifesto', 228.
[28] *SUD* 13.   [29] Ibid.

become misrelated. This misrelation Kierkegaard calls 'despair', and he holds that it is the fate not only of a few unhappy people, but is universal, though often unconscious.

This being the case, the task of human life is the attainment of a proper synthesis of the elements of rootedness and disengagement. But this is not simply a drama that is played out by each individual quite independently, in the privacy of his own soul. The proper synthesis can only be attained by the individual relating to others—to other people, but, ultimately and centrally, to God. 'The formula that describes the state of the self when despair is completely rooted out is this: in relating itself to itself, and in willing to be itself, the self rests transparently in the power that established it.'[30] Kierkegaard's account of the stages of life or spheres of existence traces in rich detail a progress through successively higher ways of life, until this final state is achieved.

Kierkegaard distinguishes three main stages: the aesthetic, the ethical, and the religious. However, on closer examination, I think we can distinguish five stages rather than the three discussed by Kierkegaard. The first of these—which might, it is true, be counted as a preliminary to the stages proper rather than as one of them—is the 'crowd life'.[31] At this stage a person identifies with his society—either with some organic community, or, worse, with the atomized, anonymous crowd that is emerging from the breakdown of traditional society. Scarcely aware of himself as an individual, he passively accepts social norms and standards as definitive of good and evil, unaware of the possibility of alternatives. The transition to the spheres of individual existence comes when the person becomes aware of himself as an individual. (Kierkegaard seems distinctly sceptical as to whether more than a handful of people ever make this transition to self-consciousness, though he often declares that he cannot be the judge of another's 'hidden inwardness'.)

The first form that this individualism can take is an asocial amoralism. The individual sees social roles and commitments as wholly alien to him. He no longer applies to himself the

[30] *SUD* 14.
[31] Kierkegaard normally treats this as a kind of aestheticism; I find it convenient here to distinguish it from the reflective form of aestheticism that Kierkegaard mostly discusses.

judgements that his society makes as to good or evil; he is interested merely in what is pleasant or unpleasant to him. This is the aesthetic stage—represented in various ways by 'A' in *Either/Or*, by Johannes the Seducer, Constantin Constantius, and the various other speakers at the banquet in *Stages on Life's Way*. These aesthetes are all highly sophisticated, reflective men; Kierkegaard does suggest that there is another sort of aesthete, who is characterized precisely by the 'immediacy' that 'A' and Johannes and Co. rather conspicuously lack. That sort of immediacy is symbolized by the figure of Don Juan, whom Kierkegaard regards as much as an unconscious force of nature as a specific person: 'Don Juan constantly hovers between being an idea, that is to say, energy, life—and being an individual.'[32] He might be described as pre-social—but the aesthetes whom Kierkegaard himself conjures up are post-social. They are free-floating individuals, possessing neither the immediacy of simple sensuality nor that of unreflective social identification. They are profoundly alienated or disengaged.

Ethical existence, the next stage, is, according to Kierkegaard, a re-engagement; the individual makes the self-conscious choice to engage in social projects, to take his place within the existing network of social institutions; he marries, takes a job and so forth, and accepts the standards of good and evil that go with social roles and institutions. But the reflective ethicist is a long way from the crowd man; he is distinguished from him by his self-consciousness. Having passed through the stage of disengagement and estrangement, he has returned to social and ethical life, but without abandoning his individuality by resuming an existence as merely a social unit. This is all reminiscent of Hegel; what is most un-Hegelian is Kierkegaard's account of the religious stage as a transcendence of the ethical, a return to individualism but on a higher level; an individualism based not on alienation from all relationships, but on the relationship between each unique individual and God. But the demands of this relationship override those deriving from all other commitments, and may require their 'teleological suspension'. Kierkegaard's dialectic of the stages of life is therefore a zigzag movement between progressively higher forms of both sociality

---

[32] *E/O* i. 91.

and individuality. The final stage that he distinguishes is 'Religiousness B' or Christianity. Especially in his last writings, he presents this in a radically individualistic and ascetic fashion, as a negation of all 'worldly' commitments. But there is a different emphasis in other of Kierkegaard's religious writings—particularly *Works of Love*. Here he argues that Christianity, having brought individuality to its highest point, then demands a thoroughly social ethics. The dialectic of the stages thus concludes with a synthesis of the two factors—social commitment and individuality—which hitherto had been played off against one another; and with each being raised to its highest intensity by the Christian demands for *agape* and for personal responsibility before God.

Of course, this is all a little bit too neat and tidy. As Kierkegaard would have been the first to acknowledge, life is more complicated than any philosophical account of it can be. One does not have to work one's way through all the stages one by one; nor can they be so sharply distinguished from one another in real life. Neither Christianity nor Religiousness A is a repudiation of the ethical; nor is the ethical a repudiation of the aesthetic. There are elements of each stage that are taken up into the next; there is no reason why a Christian need reject all that is enjoyed by an aesthete.[33] What Kierkegaard provides is a schema, an idealized account of a paradigmatic pattern of spiritual growth.

---

[33] Kierkegaard himself was ambivalent on this last point; he had a Manichaean streak which—especially towards the end of his life—tended to pull him towards presenting Christianity in a markedly ascetic fashion, as a negation of all 'wordly' values. But this outlook is untypical of the published writings from the 1840s. In 1848 Kierkegaard made a point of publishing some pieces of theatre criticism alongside his religious works, with the intention of demonstrating that he was not a formerly aesthetic writer who had turned religious, but one who had consistently maintained both aesthetic and religious interests.

2

Knowledge and Existence

In this chapter I will discuss Kierkegaard's theory of knowledge, his critique of Hegelian metaphysics, his treatment of scepticism, and his conception of subjective truth. These are not only important and interesting in themselves; they also provide a background against which to understand his ethical and religious writings. Kierkegaard's conclusion is that the purely disengaged approach to knowledge can eventually lead only to scepticism, which is not theoretically refutable, but which can only be broken with by an act of will, a refusal to accept the validity of the wholly disengaged stance. This is true of all claims to substantive (as opposed to purely formal—for example, mathematical) knowledge, but it is particularly important in the case of ethico-religious knowledge, where the stance of disengagement is wholly out of place. Here, however, a different kind of knowledge becomes possible, based not on the effort to be objective, but on a commitment to subjectivity, on passionate concern, rather than dispassionate observation.

2.1. KIERKEGAARD'S CRITIQUE OF METAPHYSICS

Kierkegaard's polemic against Hegel's 'System' is not directed so much at the detail of Hegel's arguments, as at the presuppositions and the general structure of his thought. Hence it retains a general interest and relevance apart from any particular concern with Hegel. Kierkegaard's overriding aim is to criticize the ideal of disengagement as it applies to the cognitive realm. As against all those—whether idealist metaphysicians or contemporary materialists—who claim that knowledge is, or should be, fundamentally impersonal, dispassionate, and objective, Kierkegaard insists that a thinker, no matter how objective he may try to be, remains a person, and always has the task of relating his thought to his existence as a particular individual.

No one can simply shrug off his personality, his specific nature and limitations as an individual human being, and turn himself into a pure, impersonal subject of knowledge.

One must therefore be very careful in dealing with a philosopher of the Hegelian school, and, above all, to make certain of the identity of the being with whom one has the honour to discourse. Is he a human being, an existing human being? Is he himself *sub specie aeterni*, even when he sleeps, eats, blows his nose, or whatever else a human being does? Is he himself the pure 'I am I'? This is an idea that has surely never occurred to any philosopher; but, if not, how does he stand existentially related to this entity?[1]

There are two main strands to Kierkegaard's polemic; the first is ethical. Granted that I can attempt to become objective, to adopt the stance of the 'pure knowing subject' rather than that of a concerned human being—is it right that I should do so? Is it good or desirable that I should abstract from my humanity in this way? A number of philosophers have argued that disengagement, objectivity, is the highest good. Russell writes: 'The free intellect will see as God might see, without a here and now, without hopes and fears, without the trammels of customary beliefs and traditional prejudices, calmly, dispassionately in the sole and exclusive desire of knowledge . . .'[2] In everyday life, by contrast, 'there is something feverish and confined, in comparison with which the philosophic life is calm and free'.[3]

For Kierkegaard, this attitude, which would use the impersonality of pure knowledge as a refuge from the chaos and pain of life is cowardice and escapism. To take an example that is not Kierkegaard's, Spinoza taught that the wise man ought to preserve an unshakeable serenity, based on the knowledge that everything that happens, happens by necessity and must be accepted as a manifestation of the nature of God. However, when his friend de Wit was lynched in a political riot, he reacted with furious indignation, and had to be physically prevented from rushing out to confront the mob.[4] Could this response be reconciled with his doctrine? And which does Spinoza himself more credit—the human response to tragedy, or the singularly

[1] *CUP* 271.
[2] B. Russell, *The Problems of Philosophy* (London, 1936), 248.
[3] Ibid. 244.   [4] R. J. Delahunty, *Spinoza* (London, 1985), p. xi.

inhuman philosophy (austerely impressive though, in some sense, it may be)?

Kierkegaard himself attacks the Hegelian cult of world history as demoralizing. The human, the ethical outlook is eroded by a persistent stress on objectivity, on the dispassionate investigation of cause and effect, on the grand spectacle of historical progress.

> The apprehension of the historical process . . . readily becomes a half-poetic contemplative astonishment, rather than a sober ethical perspicuity . . . it often seems as if good and evil were subject to a quantitative dialectic, and that there is a certain magnitude of crime and cunning affecting millions of individuals and entire peoples, where the ethical becomes . . . shy and diffident.

> But again and again to be absorbed in this everlasting quantification is harmful to the observer, who may easily lose the chaste purity of the ethical, which dismisses the quantitative infinitely with a sacred contempt . . .[5]

Kierkegaard's concern about the ethical effect of Hegel-inspired philosophies of history has been shown in this century to be amply justified. One thinks of the atrocities committed by Marxists, who sacrificed millions for the sake of a better future supposedly guaranteed by an 'objective' study of history.

The question, however, is not simply one of whether we are willing to accept the ethical dangers of disengagement for the sake of its cognitive advantages, for Kierkegaard is distinctly sceptical about the latter. This is the second, properly epistemo-logical, strand of his critique. It is not the case that Kierkegaard—as is sometimes claimed by admirers as well as critics—simply rejects reason, science, or the attempt to think objectively. Of course the scholar must abstract from his personal feelings and concerns in order to arrive at an accurate and unprejudiced view of what he is investigating. 'No, all honour to the pursuits of science . . . but the ethical is, and remains the highest task for every human being.'[6] Kierkegaard has no objection to science and scholarship as such. What he does insist on reminding us is that a scientist is a human being before he is a scientist, and therefore that the ethical task of self-realization has priority over the task of science. Kierkegaard's objection is not to science but to the attempt to confuse the ethical and the existential with

---

[5] *CUP* 127.   [6] Ibid. 135.

pseudo-scientific formulae, to turn the limited degree of abstraction from personal interests that is necessary for science into a philosophy, which aims to see all phenomena, all occurrences, with the same dispassionate objectivity. 'When . . . a tumultuous scientist seeks to invade the sphere of the existential, and there proceeds to confuse the ethical, . . . then he is as scientist no faithful lover, and science itself stands ready to deliver him up to a comic apprehension.'[7] 'Comic', because there is a kind of absurdity in a mere human being claiming to see things 'as God might see them', and being so 'absent-minded' as to forget or to overlook as beneath his dignity the ethical problems of his personal existence.

Kierkegaard makes a distinction between what he calls 'pure' and 'abstract' thought. The latter he characterizes in these terms: 'The way of objective reflection leads to abstract thought, to mathematics, to historical knowledge of different kinds; and always it leads away from the subject, whose existence or non-existence, and, from the objective point of view quite rightly, becomes infinitely indifferent.'[8] 'Abstract thought', then, is the thought of the scientist or scholar who attempts to gain an objective understanding of the phenomena he studies—one that will be valid for any investigator, one that makes no essential reference to his own personality. Now, for Kierkegaard, this sort of thinking is valid so long as it realizes its own limits, and does not tempt the thinker to forget his own subjectivity. In fact, a good deal of philosophy since Kierkegaard's time has been concerned to show that—even in mathematics and physics, and still more in 'human sciences' such as history—a thinker always starts with his particular situation and background, and can never wholly escape from them.[9] However, a degree of objectivity, of abstraction from the personal, is clearly necessary for science and scholarship, and, as we have seen, Kierkegaard does not oppose this. The risk is, however, that the abstract thinker will forget his limitations, and abstract too far. When this happens, we move from science to metaphysics, from

---

[7] *CUP* 136.   [8] Ibid. 173.
[9] I am thinking of the work of Merleau-Ponty and of the later Wittgenstein, for instance; also Gadamer's hermeneutics, which attacks the Enlightenment's attempt to free thinking from 'prejudice', and sees 'prejudices' instead as the necessary starting-point of thought.

abstract to 'pure' thought. Kierkegaard describes the difference thus: 'Abstract thought is disinterested . . . but pure thought is altogether detached, and not like the abstract thought that does indeed abstract from existence, but nevertheless preserves a relationship to it.'[10]

The legitimate scientist makes a limited abstraction from his personal outlook in order to focus objectively on certain phenomena. The pure thinker aims to understand the whole of reality objectively as 'a system'. To do this, he requires a much greater degree of abstraction. The scientist is simply a human being exercising one particular human capacity—for objective thinking. The metaphysician in the bad sense (Kierkegaard does not deny that there can be a good sense, a more modest kind of metaphysics) aims to shrug off his humanity altogether, to transform himself into a pure knowing subject who, having abstracted himself from the limits of his finitude, is able to see the world 'as God might', to see all phenomena cohering in a rationally intelligible system. Kierkegaard insists that this cannot be done. He presents two theses: '(A), a logical system is possible; (B), an existential system is impossible.'[11] Knowledge can be certain and complete only where it is purely formal; substantive knowledge is always fragmentary, limited, and provisional.

A logical system is possible, Kierkegaard claims, but only on the condition that 'Nothing . . . be incorporated in a logical system that has any relation to existence, that is not indifferent to existence.'[12] A purely formal logic may be drawn up; so may a discussion of what is implied by certain concepts once initial definitions have been given. But nothing is shown thereby as to how this logical system relates to reality. Kierkegaard draws a very sharp distinction between logic and language on the one hand, and reality or existence on the other. In his early, unfinished work *Johannes Climacus* he states: 'The moment I make a statement about reality, contradiction is present, for what I say is ideality.'[13] One might object to the use of the word 'contradiction' in this formula, but Kierkegaard's point is that the statement I make, when considered from the point of view of its semantic content, is a proposition, a logical entity, and not

---

[10] *CUP* 278.   [11] Ibid. 99.
[12] Ibid. 100.   [13] *JC* 168.

itself an element of existence. Language, with its inherent generality, can never grasp the particularity of things, but leads us away into the realm of ideality, of generalization.

'Existence . . . is a difficult category to deal with; for if I think it, I abrogate it, and then I do not think it.'[14] What I think is the thought of existence—not existence itself. This may seem an elementary point, but various philosophies—including Hegel's—have been founded on the effort to ignore it. Hegel regarded existence as an embodiment of the relation between categories, and thus attempted to make his logic a system that would be at once logical and existential. But the attempt produces on the one hand 'a sheer confusion of logical science',[15] and on the other a confusion of thought about the empirically real world, where the physical relation of causation gets hopelessly muddled up with the logical relationship between premiss and conclusion.[16]

Kierkegaard will not permit any attempt to think of reality as a whole, as though we could stand outside it. Certainly we can think about reality, but we cannot convert it into a system, produce a complete systematic account that would explain everything. Immersed in the flux of time, of 'becoming', I cannot transcend my limits so as to see things absolutely. This does not mean that Kierkegaard adopts some version of relativism or perspectivism, according to which there is no independently real world, no way things really are, apart from our knowledge of them. But it is only God who can enjoy this absolute point of view. 'An existential system cannot be formulated. Does this mean that no such system exists? By no means; nor is this implied in our assertion. Reality itself is a system—for God; but it cannot be a system for any existing spirit. System and finality correspond to one another, but existence is precisely the opposite of finality.'[17]

This brings us to Kierkegaard's discussion of truth. He contrasts the 'empirical' theory—truth as 'the conformity of thought and being' (what is usually called the 'correspondence theory' of truth)—and the 'idealistic' theory—truth as 'the

---

[14] *CUP* 274.   [15] Ibid. 99.

[16] Cf. *PhF* 73–5. This objection to the transition from logic to reality underlies Kierkegaard's criticism not only of Hegel, but of the Cartesian *Cogito* and of the ontological argument for the existence of God (*CUP* 281 and 298).

[17] *CUP* 107.

conformity of being with thought'.[18] This latter theory—Hegel's basically—considers things to be true in so far as they conform fully to their essences, which are defined in logic. Kierkegaard will not, of course, permit this confusion of logic and existence. In so far as it means anything, the 'idealistic' formula reduces to a tautology. 'Thought and being mean one and the same thing, and the correspondence spoken of is merely an abstract self-identity.'[19] That is, 'being' ceases to refer to empirical reality, and comes to mean merely 'the abstract reflection of, or the abstract prototype for, what being is as concrete empirical being.'[20] Being is thus reduced to the thought of being, so, naturally, it conforms to thought. But this is empty.

We are therefore left with the 'empirical' correspondence theory, according to which a statement is true if it corresponds to the reality that it purports to describe. Kierkegaard does not object to this definition, but he points out that in this case 'truth is at once transformed into a *desideratum*, and everything must be understood in terms of becoming; for the empirical object is unfinished and the existing cognitive spirit is itself in process of becoming. Thus the truth becomes an approximation . . .'[21] No empirical statement is ever wholly certain, is ever—as the logical positivists were eventually forced to admit—capable of conclusive verification. However sure I may be of something at the moment, I can never be sure that something may not happen the next minute which would force me to change my mind. I may be quite certain that I am now watching a cat walking across the room. But it is always possible that, at the next moment, it may suddenly expand to an enormous size or start talking to me. It may turn out to be a cunningly contrived robot, a hologram, an alien from another galaxy. And this is true of scientific hypotheses as well as of everyday statements. 'An assumption might very well explain a great many cases, and thereby confirm its own truth, and yet later appear to be untrue as soon as something happens it cannot explain.'[22]

---

[18] Ibid. 169.   [19] Ibid. 170.   [20] Ibid.   [21] Ibid. 169.
[22] *W of L* 185. This whole section of *Works of Love* is very interesting, as showing the existential and ethical use that Kierkegaard makes of an apparently abstract epistemological principle. The argument is that, because nothing is objectively certain, I can always put a different interpretation on someone's behaviour. The loving person, while not naïve—he is well aware of the

Kierkegaard's conception of truth as approximative, as a desideratum, has parallels with the ideas of some contemporary philosophers such as Putnam, for whom 'truth' is an ideal or regulative concept, representing an ideal—but never attained—end-point of enquiry. I think Kierkegaard differs from this outlook in that he maintains that there is absolute truth; but this is known only to God. God sees absolutely how things are, but human beings have only a partial, limited, perspectival knowledge. For us to aspire to a 'God's-eye view' is, for Kierkegaard, both blasphemous and comic in its absurdity.

Disengaged, abstract thought, whatever its value, does not lead to absolute or certain knowledge. Human knowledge remains provisional and partial. However, one may see this clearly, but still insist on the disengaged stance. The result of this is scepticism, a topic that Kierkegaard discusses with profundity and originality.

2.2. KNOWLEDGE, SCEPTICISM, AND THE WILL

In everyday life we take all sorts of things for granted—that the things we see around us really do exist independently of us, that the sun will rise tomorrow, that other people have thoughts and feelings, are not merely automata. This is the natural, pre-reflective outlook. But we can stand back from our natural beliefs, 'suspending' or 'bracketing' them, while asking if we really do have rational grounds for believing such things. This was the practice of Descartes, who aimed to doubt whatever could be doubted, in order to strip away our pre-reflective beliefs, before reconstructing knowledge on the basis of rational, objectively tested certainty. Much recent philosophy has contested this programme of Descartes, arguing that we cannot really abstract from our everyday beliefs, and that it is an illusion to think that they can, or should, be brought before the tribunal of a wholly disengaged rational intelligence. Nevertheless, once the process of disengagement from such 'natural'

possibility of more cynical interpretations—chooses to put the most generous possible interpretation on anyone's actions, to see them in the best light he can. Knowledge in itself is objective and, therefore, hypothetical; it is for the existing individual to choose whether to interpret the facts cynically or 'lovingly'.

beliefs as that the sun orbits the earth, or that the earth is flat, has started, it seems hard to see why it should be halted at any one particlar point. As I argued in Chapter 1.1, the ideal of disengagement has come to enjoy a central role in our culture. We are all strongly influenced by the idea that we should only hold a belief if it can be justified rationally—not by appeals to authority, or to natural inclination, or common sense, or to our emotional needs and wants, but to a dispassionate, detached intellect.

Now, if Kierkegaard is right, this sort of abstract thought cannot attain certain knowledge of reality. If we make the initial movement of disengagement from our ordinary beliefs, we can succeed in calling them into question; but abstract thought does not have the capacity to reconstruct knowledge on the basis of objective certainty. One may perform the limited abstraction of the scientist or scholar, still 'preserving a relation to' existence, and not attempting a general critique or suspension of everyday belief. But if one performs the more general and radical abstraction of the metaphysician, this will not lead to a deeper, more securely grounded knowledge. One is then faced with a dilemma: abandon disengagement and accept ordinary knowledge-claims; or retain the disengaged stance and embrace scepticism. This parallels very closely the dilemma of the post-Kantian moralist, mentioned in Chapter 1.1: abandon disengagement for the sake of a substantive ethic; or retain disengagement and accept some form of moral subjectivism.

In *Johannes Climacus*, as we have seen, Kierkegaard makes a sharp distinction between 'ideality' (logic, language) and 'reality'. In itself, reality just is; things are not true or false in themselves. But neither does the question of truth or falsity arise when language and logic are just regarded by themselves, apart from any relation to reality—as logicians regard their closed deductive systems, or as structuralists regard language, seeing it as an autonomous network in which the elements are defined according to their internal relationships rather than by their reference to extralinguistic realities. 'In ideality, everything is just as perfectly true as in reality . . . not until the moment that ideality is brought into relation with reality does possibility appear.'[23]

---

[23] *JC* 168.

Reality and ideality are brought into contact through consciousness. Kierkegaard suggests, indeed, that consciousness can be defined as the relating of reality and ideality.[24] This relation is twofold: 'Insofar as what was said is supposed to be an expression of reality, I have brought this into relation with ideality; insofar as what was said is something produced by me, I have brought ideality into relation with reality.'[25] In other words, by using language to talk about something, I relate it to 'ideality'—that is, to the general categories under which I subsume the thing. But I also bring the generality of language down to 'reality' by performing a particular speech-act in a particular situation, using general expressions to refer—in the context of my act—to a particular thing.

It is here that the possibility of doubt appears. For the relating of ideality and reality creates the possibility of a misrelation. Has my thought, my statement, accurately expressed reality? Are things really as I say they are? However exhaustive my investigations, the possibility of doubt can never be eliminated. Thus, to make any statement—other than a purely formal one— is to take a cognitive risk. In the *Fragments* Kierkegaard characterizes scepticism as a refusal to take such risks. 'The Greek sceptic did not deny the correctness of sensation and of immediate cognition, but, said he, error has an utterly different basis—it comes from the conclusions I draw. If I can only avoid drawing conclusions, I shall never be deceived.'[26] He gives an example: 'belief . . . does not believe that the star exists, for that it sees, but it believes that the star has come into existence.'[27] What the sceptic is determined to avoid is belief in this sense; he accepts what his senses show him, but he draws no conclusions, and is therefore never deceived. 'If, for example, sensation shows me in the distance a round object that close at hand is seen to be square, or shows me a stick that looks broken in the

---

[24] *JC* 168. One might compare this with Popper's idea that the main function of what he calls 'World 2' (consciousness) is to mediate between 'World 1' (physical reality) and 'World 3' (the realm of languages, theories, and of 'objective knowledge').   [25] Ibid.   [26] *PhF* 82.

[27] Ibid. 81. Kierkegaard here seems to overlook his own earlier point that language always takes us beyond the sensory given. To identify an object as 'a star' is already to think of it as an entity of a definite kind with a temporal history. I do not think that this affects Kierkegaard's substantive point—it just shows that he could have made it more radically.

water although it is straight when taken out, sensation has not deceived me, but I am deceived only when I conclude something about that stick and that object.'[28]

Regarded in this way, scepticism is not a purely intellectual position; it is an attitude of the will. 'Greek scepticism was a withdrawing scepticism; they doubted not by virtue of knowledge but by virtue of will. This implies that doubt can be terminated only in freedom, by an act of will, something every Greek sceptic would understand . . . but he would not terminate his scepticism, precisely because he willed to doubt.'[29] This is, I think, fundamentally right as an account of scepticism. After sceptical doubts have been raised in respect of any proposition, I can still choose my attitude: either take the cognitive risk of committing myself to a definite belief, or suspend judgement. Scepticism does not, of course, tell us that we are mistaken in thinking *x*; it's really *y*. That would simply be rejecting one knowledge-claim for another. What scepticism does tell us is that *x* may be mistaken; and so may *y*. It then remains up to us to choose nevertheless to believe *x* or *y*, or to suspend judgement between them. But this is a matter of choice, of decision, of will.[30]

What follows from this is that scepticism cannot be refuted, but only rejected. If scepticism itself is an attitude of will, so too is anti-scepticism. 'The conclusion of belief is no conclusion but a resolution, and thus doubt is excluded.'[31] The attempt to refute scepticism on the purely intellectual level is wholly mistaken. As we have seen, thought, for Kierkegaard, can never attain any certainty in existential matters; it can only find certainty in purely formal or deductive reasoning. And this has only a

---

[28] Ibid. 82–3.   [29] Ibid. 82.

[30] Though it was a disengaged position, Greek scepticism was not 'absent-minded'—the sceptics did not simply forget their existence as particular human beings, or suppose that they could abstract from it at the snap of a finger. Greek scepticism was a will to disengagement, and therefore an existential attitude. 'The so-called ataraxy of the sceptics was therefore an existential attempt to abstract from existence. In our time the process of abstacting from existence has been relegated to the printed page . . .' (*CUP* 282). Kierkegaard considered that this was true of the Greek metaphysicians also; for them, to become objective was a lifelong struggle to rise beyond the particularity of their natural viewpoint. It was not a pose that they could adopt when entering the lecture-room and leave behind when they went out (which was—whether justly or not—Kierkegaard's accusation against the Hegelians of his day).   [31] *PhF* 84.

'hypothetical'[32] relation to existence; the sceptical doubt arises precisely when we try, not hypothetically, but actually, to relate thought to existence, asserting that particular categories do apply to something real. Given that scepticism only arises when we try to apply thought to the contingencies of empirical reality, it is not possible to refute it beforehand in thought. Descartes's *Cogito* was supposed to establish that I cannot doubt my own existence, hence there is at least this existential certainty before which doubt must halt. Kierkegaard is not impressed; the trouble is that the 'I' whose existence is asserted in the argument 'I think, therefore I am', remains no more than a conceptual posit, an abstract subject of thought, not a concrete individual.[33] Some critics of Descartes would not allow even this much; Lichtenberg and others argued that the only assertion Descartes should have made was that 'there is thought', without reference to a thinking subject. Possibly, Kierkegaard did not follow this line of thought because he was impressed by Kant's argument that 'it must be possible for the "I think" to accompany all my representations'.[34] But even this Kantian 'I think' is a purely conceptual, rather than a concrete, empirical being. We are brought no closer to real existence.

Nor is Kierkegaard convinced by the argument that scepticism is self-refuting, for the sceptic at least must assert that there is one thing he knows for certain—that nothing is certain. The sceptic does not need to assert this; he may well state that he is uncertain whether certain knowledge is possible or not. Or he may simply refuse to make any general statements of this kind, and confine himself to criticizing each particular knowledge-claim as it arises.[35] As Kierkegaard says, 'he has no results, not even negative ones (for this would mean the acknowledgement of knowledge) but by the power of the will he decides to restrain himself and hold himself back . . . from any conclusion.'[36]

---

[32] *CUP* 100–1.   [33] Ibid. 281.

[34] I. Kant, *Critique of Pure Reason*, trans. N. Kemp Smith (London, 1982), B131.

[35] Sextus Empiricus gives the classical sceptics' answer to this criticism: 'In determining nothing, the Sceptic does not even determine the very formula "I determine nothing". [Rather] he means this: "My state of mind at the present is such that I make no dogmatic affirmation or denial of anything falling under the present investigation." ' (Sextus Empiricus, *Selections from the Major Writings on Scepticism, Man and God*, ed. P. Hallie (Indianapolis, 1985), 83.)

[36] *PhF* 85.

There is, then, at the basis of all substantive knowledge, an attitude of will, a willingness to commit oneself to what is dubitable. Kierkegaard is not arguing that a conscious act of will underlies all our everyday beliefs. Of course, I do not make a conscious decision to exclude sceptical doubt every time I identify something as a cat or a star. We are not required by some intellectual necessity to start with scepticism—Kierkegaard states his preference for the Greek idea that philosophy begins with wonder, rather than the modern (Cartesian) idea that it begins with doubt. But once the sceptical possibility has been raised, it cannot be refuted on its own terms, at the level of the disengaged intellect. It can only be rejected, broken with, by a decision of the will. And this means a decision against disengagement, a decision to accept that substantive knowledge is dubitable, and that it is merely human knowledge, the knowledge that is available to a limited finite creature. Once we choose to abstract from our limits, to attempt to transcend our finitude, we make substantive knowledge impossible, for we impose the condition that it must be demonstrated with certainty to a disengaged intelligence. And this condition cannot be met. The choice remains: to stand back from our natural inclination to believe, from our natural willingness to take things for granted, and insist on sceptical suspension of judgement; or to make the decision to thrust aside the possibility of doubt, and re-engage with our natural, pre-reflective certainties. What Kierkegaard reminds us is that this is a choice. The ideal of disengaged objectivity is too deeply rooted in our culture for us simply to shrug it off as absurd or to dismiss the demand for objectivity as simply mistaken. Underlying all knowledge, then, there is, for Kierkegaard, an existential attitude—a will to believe, in spite of the possibility of doubt.

In the section that follows, I want to develop further and to defend the Kierkegaardian ideas about scepticism that I have outlined here, and to show their relevance to issues discussed in contemporary philosophy. I shall do this by a consideration of modern meaning-scepticism. Philosophy in this century has tended to focus especially on language (this is true of 'Continental' as well as of 'analytic' philosophy), and so the characteristic modern form of scepticism is scepticism about language, about what—if anything—meaning is. I shall discuss two versions of meaning-scepticism: one deriving from the work of Quine and Davidson, the other from French post-structuralism, particularly Derrida. I will then say something about the later work of Wittgenstein. This has been interpreted by Kripke as involving a form of radical meaning-scepticism; I see it more as a critical response to such scepticism, one that shows interesting similarities to Kierkegaard's thought, as well as differences. The aim of my discussion will be to support the two main theses advanced so far; that scepticism results from the adoption of the disengaged stance; and that the rejection of scepticism is an act of will rather than a purely intellectual operation.

2.3. SCEPTICISM AND LANGUAGE

2.3.1. *Quine and Davidson*

Quine is a radical materialist, and he wishes to produce an account of language from a materialist point of view. This involves him taking up an externalist stance—the scientific investigator of language, as of anything else, proceeds by looking in, from the outside, at the phenomena to be accounted for. Quine is committed to denying that there is any such thing as inherently participative knowledge. Knowledge is what can be attained by the dispassionate scientific observer, standing outside the phenomena he observes. Hence his commitment to an extensionalist account of language, for, as Ramberg has put it, 'If we are extensionalists about meaning we cannot imagine what it is for language to have an "inside".'[37] Quine's commitment to the disengaged stance is most vividly expressed by his doctrine of the indeterminacy of translation. As the paradigm of linguistic understanding, he takes the predicament of an explorer who stumbles upon some hitherto unknown people, and tries to decypher, from scratch, their wholly unfamiliar language.

It is crucial to realize that Quine is not just discussing translation; he is using the situation of the radical translator as a dramatic illustration of the nature of all linguistic understanding. 'On deeper reflection, radical translation begins at home. Must

[37] B. Ramberg, *Donald Davidson's Philosophy of Language* (Oxford, 1989), 120.

we equate our neighbours' English words with the same string of phonemes in our own mouths? Certainly not . . . The problem at home differs none from radical translation ordinarily so called, except in the wilfulness of this suspension of homophonic translation.'[38] This is surely one of the most powerful images of the disengaged self to have been produced in modern thought. In trying to understand the noises coming out of our neighbours' mouths, each of us is fundamentally in the same position as an anthropologist listening to a wholly unfamiliar language being used. Quine is not, of course, arguing that we should normally suspend the homophonic rule in 'translating' our neighbours' speech. But it is possible to do so, and, for Quine, there is no content to the intuitive idea that by so doing, we would lose access to a real knowledge of meanings, over and above that which is available to the radical translator.

Attempting to outline the understanding of language that can be obtained from this external, observational stance, Quine is led largely to dismiss the concept of meaning as we intuitively use it. He does allow that there are some utterances that can be given 'stimulus-meaning' by correlating them with the sensory stimulations occurring at the times at which they would be assented to or dissented from; but this really represents all the empirical sense that we can make of the notion of meaning. 'Stimulus-meaning . . . falls short in various ways of one's intuitive demands on "meaning" . . . Yet stimulus-meaning, by whatever name, may be properly looked upon still as the objective reality that the linguist has to probe when he undertakes radical translation.'[39] Accordingly, Quine offers us 'not behaviouristic reconstructions of intuitive semantics, but only a behaviouristic ersatz'.[40] From the 'objective' standpoint of the behaviourist, all that really happens—the only basic, hard facts there are—is that organisms emit certain noises in response to certain stimuli. Our natural belief that these noises embody 'meanings' is a pre-scientific illusion. Once we leave the restricted ground of stimulus-meaning, there is no determinate,

[38] W. V. Quine, 'Ontological Relativity', in his *Ontological Relativity and Other Essays* (New York, 1969), 46–7.
[39] W. V. Quine, *Word and Object* (Cambridge, Mass., 1960), 39.
[40] Ibid. 66.

'objective reality' of real meaning to which our translations must conform: 'The arbitrariness of reading our objectifications into the heathen speech reflects not so much the inscrutability of the heathen mind, as that there is nothing to scrute.'[41]

If the notion of meaning is empty and pre-scientific, this does not apply merely to the 'heathen', but to my neighbours and even to myself. 'If there is really no fact of the matter, then the inscrutability of reference can be brought even closer to home than the neighbours' case; we can apply it to ourselves.'[42] Normally, when talking to our neighbours or when engaged in internal monologue, we assume that the sounds we make are the embodiment of meanings. We simply hear our own language as meaningful. But, for Quine, scientific rigour requires that we adopt—towards our neighbours and even towards ourselves—the disengaged, objective stance that he dramatically represents with the figure of the radical translator. Objectively, there simply is no more to language than people's tendencies to produce certain sounds in response to certain stimuli. 'There are no meanings, nor likenesses, nor distinctions of meaning, beyond what are implicit in people's dispositions to overt behaviour.'[43] Meaningful language, as we normally think of it, simply disappears.

Quine thinks of himself as attempting to give an objective, scientific account of language. I would like to argue that this is simply not possible. The knowledge of language is an inherently participative knowledge. Charles Taylor notes that 'to understand a language you need to understand the social life and outlook of those who speak it . . . And you cannot understand a form of life as a pure detached observer.'[44] He goes on to describe as an 'absurdity . . . Quine's notion that any understanding of one person's language by another is the application of a theory. As though we could ever understand each other if we stood to each other in the stance of observers.'[45] If, as I believe, Taylor is right about this, then there is a kind of knowledge that is actually lost or made impossible by the adoption of the purely observational stance. Quine's own attempt to provide a scientific account of

[41] W. V. Quine, 'Speaking of Objects', in *Ontological Relativity*, 5.
[42] Quine, 'Ontological Relativity', 47.   [43] Ibid. 29.
[44] C. Taylor, 'Theories of Meaning', in *Human Agency and Language* (Philosophical Papers, 1; Cambridge, 1985), 281.   [45] Ibid. 281–2.

language from this detached standpoint should not, I think, be taken particularly seriously; it shares the general absurdity of behaviourism. Despite his scientific intentions, Quine's significance is as the proponent of a new form of scepticism. The stance of disengagement does not make possible a deeper, objective knowledge of language; it does destroy our everyday understanding of language as participants in it. We may reject this scepticism about meaning by refusing to adopt the observational stance; but this is not a pure intellectual conclusion, but a commitment to a shared intuitive sense of meaning.

Similar comments apply to Davidson's philosophy of language. There are important differences between Davidson and Quine, but Davidson shares Quine's crucial assumptions that language is to be understood from an external, detached perspective, and that such understanding should take the form of a theory. He, too, excludes the natural participative knowledge that we have as language-users, and, although his 'radical interpretation' is not the same as Quine's 'radical translation', he adopts Quine's myth of the explorer discovering a strange tribe as illustrating the fundamental nature of linguistic understanding. 'The problem of interpretation is domestic as well as foreign; it surfaces for speakers of the same language in the form of the question, how can it be determined that the language is the same? . . . all understanding of the speech of another involves radical interpretation.'[46]

Davidson is not a behaviourist, and has no wish to delete references to beliefs and desires from his theoretical apparatus. But his stance is still that of the detached observer, noticing organisms emitting noises. To make sense of these, he attempts to impose upon them a theoretical structure which will allow each statement made in the language under examination to be matched with an equivalent statement in a metalanguage (which may be the same or different). But the resulting ascription of meanings to words is a piece of revisable theoretical machinery, which does not reflect any fact of the matter as to what words actually do mean. 'We compensate for the paucity of evidence concerning the meanings of individual sentences, not by trying to produce evidence for the meanings

[46] D. Davidson, 'Radical Interpretation', in his *Inquiries into Truth and Interpretation* (Oxford, 1984), 125.

of words, but by considering the evidence for a theory of the language to which the sentence belongs. Words, and one or another way of connecting them with objects, are constructs we need to implement the theory.'[47]

This holistic model of language, shared by Quine and Davidson, can only seem plausible to one who thinks of himself as observing language from the outside. It fails to explain how the language could be learned or actually used. Arguing against Quine, Dummett notes: 'A thoroughgoing holism, while it may provide an abstractly intelligible model of language, fails to give a credible account either of how we use language as an instrument of communication, or of how we acquire a mastery of language.'[48] The notion that linguistic understanding involves the construction of a theory is a curious piece of over-intellectualism; I have a knowledge of the English language, but my beliefs as to the meanings of most of the English words that I know are certainly not theoretical hypotheses to be revised in the light of further evidence. I know what the words I use mean; nor is there any 'paucity' in my 'evidence' for the meanings of individual sentences.

It is a striking tribute to the power of the philosophical myths of objectivity and disengagement that Davidson should have neglected such platitudinous but obvious truths about language in order to pursue the chimera of an objective theory. Though he is less crudely reductive than Quine, Davidson also ends up by denying our everyday linguistic knowledge and by making meanings into theoretical constructs. This outlook is hardly less sceptical than Quine's. Once we have made the effort to disengage from our intuitive understanding of language, sceptical doubts arise easily. Is my neighbour really speaking the same language as me? How should I interpret those noises he is making? Should I have a different interpretative theory for each of my neighbours? (In his recent work Davidson has come to reject the concept of language itself as useless; each new utterance that I hear is the occasion for a new feat of interpretation.) Davidson, like Quine, is best regarded not as making any positive contribution to linguistic knowledge, but as

[47] D. Davidson, 'Reality without Reference', in *Inquiries into Truth and Interpretation*, 225.

[48] M. Dummett, *Frege: Philosophy of Language*, 2nd edn. (London, 1978), 597–8.

developing a form of radical scepticism. From the perspective of disengagement, the concept of meaning vanishes altogether. We have the choice: disengaged scepticism, or a knowledge that is inherently participative and which therefore cannot claim to be objective in the strong sense. This will be made clearer by a discussion of an intellectual tradition very different in style from that of Quine and Davidson, but which has produced some curiously similar results—that of French 'post-structuralism'.

2.3.2. Derrida

Stylistically, there is an enormous difference between the sober, analytical approach of Quine or Davidson, with their use of formal logic and their austere concern with the exact sciences, and that of the French post-structuralists, with their rather self-consciously 'playful' and sometimes Joycean prose, and their concern with politics, poetics, and psychoanalysis. But in both cases we see a stress on the disengaged subject leading to a radical scepticism about meaning. It might initially seem strange to describe post-structuralism as a philosophy of the disengaged subject; the structuralists established themselves on the French cultural scene by polemicizing against the phenomenological 'philosophy of the subject', and the post-structuralists only intensified this critique. But—as with materialism and its reduction of subjectivity to brain-processes—the pure subject is pushed out of the 'objective' world only to reappear—unacknowledged—as the presupposition of the objectivist discourse. In materialism the pure subject returns in the form of the detached scientific observer; in post-structuralism it takes on the more characteristically French guise of the bohemian free spirit who has seen through the illusions and hypocrisies of the bourgeoisie. In what follows, I shall concentrate on Derrida, though rather similar conclusions can be drawn from the works of Barthes, Foucault, Lyotard, and others.

Derrida, though influenced by the phenomenological tradition, rejects Husserl's subjectivist philosophy of language, which traces meaning back to the activity of the pure ego. With Barthes and others, he proclaims the 'Death of the Author'—the end of the belief that a text is given a single determinate meaning by the intentions of its author. But the Death of the Author means the Birth of the Interpreter. We may pass from the disengagement of the metaphysician to that of the sceptic; from the belief in the author as absolute subject, his mental intentions determining the meaning of the text, to the belief that texts have no determinate meanings—and that, therefore, the interpreter becomes totally free, detached from all constraints, and able to follow up an indefinite number of possible interpretations, none of which is more valid than any of the others. In a sense that has more parallels with Davidson's than one might at first suspect, Derrida seems to license[49] a practice of 'radical interpretation', in which the interpreter abandons the project of finding the meaning of a text, and treats it instead as a pre-text for his own displays of virtuosity in multiplying different interpretations. Radically disengaged, suspending his natural tendencies to see texts as embodying meanings, the Derridean interpreter abstracts his texts from the external reality to which we would normally think of them as referring. '[R]eading . . . cannot legitimately transgress the text toward something other than it, toward a referent . . . There is nothing outside the text.'[50] Nor can interpretation consist in an appeal to authorial intentions. The text is an autonomous system, but one in which many different interpretative patterns may be discovered (or created).

Following Saussure, Derrida sees the meaning of signs as given by their relations to other signs rather than to anything 'outside the text'. But Derrida will not concede that context places determinate limits on the possible ways of relating one word to others in a language. Hence it is impossible for a writer to decide to use a word to mean something definite—he cannot control language in that way. The word retains an indefinite range of possible meanings, some of which are actualized when an interpreter chooses to relate it to a particular group of other words. 'The meaning of meaning . . . is infinite implication,

---

[49] I am being slightly cautious here. Derrida is a very obscure and very elusive writer. He also seems sometimes to be pursuing a double strategy—making outrageous claims so as to seem radical and exciting, and then much more sober ones so as to seem intellectually respectable. In any case, the interpretation that I have given here represents the way in which Derrida has been widely understood, even if this does not accord with his intentions. (But can Derrida, in any case, consistently claim that the meaning of his texts can be determined by reference to his intentions?)

[50] J. Derrida, *Of Grammatology*, trans. G. C. Spivak (Baltimore and London, 1974), 158.

the indefinite referral of signifier to signifier . . . its force is a certain pure and infinite equivocality which gives signified meaning no respite, no rest, but engages it in its own economy so that it always signifies again and differs.'[51] Nor can any particular text be isolated from the whole system of the language in which it is written. In his commentary on Plato's *Phaedrus* Derrida remarks: 'Like any text, the text of "Plato" couldn't not be involved, at least in a virtual, dynamic, lateral manner, with all the words that comprised the system of the Greek language. Certain forces of association unite . . . the words "actually present" in a discourse with all the other words in the lexical system, whether or not they appear as "words".'[52]

This holistic attitude to language is reminiscent of Quine and Davidson, and open to the same fundamental objection—that it cannot account for the learning or use of a language. If I cannot understand any word in a language as having any determinate meaning without considering its relations to all the other words in the language, then it is hard to see how I could ever begin to learn the language, and hard to see how I could ever use it to say anything definite.

Derrida's disengaged, externalist approach is what underlies his account of language as writing. In criticizing the supposed tendency of Western thought to treat speech as prior to writing, he is not, of course, denying the obvious facts that we learn to speak before we learn to write, and that, for most of human history, most people have been illiterate. But his argument is that all language turns out to have the characteristics that have been ascribed to writing in the attempt to differentiate it from speech. In writing, the fundamental nature of all language is made clear. Seeing a written text that may originally have been produced by an author who has been dead for centuries, I am forced to realize that the text has an autonomous existence; it is not given its true meaning by the intentions of an author, and it is up to me to find what meaning I can in it. But this is also the case with speech, though it is easier to overlook it and to suppose that the meaning of someone's verbal utterances is conclusively guaranteed by the pure mental ideas in the speaker's head. But

---

[51] J. Derrida, 'Force and Signification', in his *Writing and Difference*, trans. A. Bass (London, 1978), 25.
[52] J. Derrida, *Dissemination*, trans. B. Johnson (London, 1981), 129–30.

language is never controllable by the subject in this way. 'For the written to be the written, it must continue to "act" and to be legible, even if what is called the author of the writing no longer answers for what he has written, [and] . . . in general, he does not support, with his absolutely current and present intention or attention, the plenitude of his meaning . . .'[53]

Derrida goes on to point out that 'This essential drifting, due to writing as an iterative structure cut off from all absolute responsibility, from consciousness as the authority of the last analysis, writing orphaned and separated at birth from the assistance of its father, is indeed what Plato condemned in the *Phaedrus*.'[54] But such condemnations are in vain; what Plato took to be the specific characteristics of writing are the essential characteristics of all language.

No doubt Derrida is right to stress that language pre-exists the language-user, and is never simply a medium for the conveyance of his pre-linguistic meanings and ideas. But he fails to do justice to the fact that, nevertheless, texts are still produced by particular human beings in order to convey their thoughts. I may not be the absolute source of my meanings in a metaphysical or transcendental sense, but this does not stop me from being responsible for the meaning of what I say and write in an everyday sense. From Derrida's disengaged perspective, meaning either exists as an absolute, knowable from that perspective, or else it collapses altogether, evaporating in the free play of interpretation. What he neglects is the realm in which meaning is created and preserved in everyday action and interaction. The practical functions of language, which are what place limits on the freedom of interpretation and allow for the relative stability of meaning, are largely overlooked by Derrida.

Granted that we should avoid a sharp dualism between speech and writing, this may be done in different ways. There is a great difference between seeing someone's speech as though it were a text that I am unconstrained in interpreting, and in seeing a text as though it were someone's speech, where I am trying to understand what someone else has to say, to open

---

[53] J. Derrida, 'Signature Event Context', in his *Margins of Philosophy*, trans. A. Bass (Brighton, 1982), 316.
[54] Ibid.

myself to his meaning. For Derrida, language is to be understood on the model of a solitary reader of a 'literary' text following up various trains of association that strike him. Language as a means of communication, where a large measure of consensus and agreement as to meaning is essential, seems to drop out. It would be possible to produce a deconstructive reading of a technical manual, but no one does it; its meaning is rendered determinate in practice because of its context, which is to serve and guide practical activity. In his discussions of Austin and Searle, Derrida denies that context can determine meaning, can set a limit to its 'dissemination'. For no one can set limits to what may be treated as the relevant context; interpreters may produce radically different interpretations of a text by setting it in different contexts. It is true that, in theory, there is no clear cut-off point, and, therefore, no end to the possible elaboration of context. But language is used by human beings in concrete, practical situations, and practice is what sets limits to the specification of context.

It is by taking language away from practice, away from its role in human interaction (this is the deepest meaning of his interpretation of language as writing), that Derrida produces his radical scepticism.[55] And it is only by seeing language as a medium of practical interaction that this scepticism can be overcome. I believe that this holds good for the interpretation of a poem as much as it does for the interpretation of a technical manual; the poem, too, is to be treated as a communication from another person that can help us to understand our world, and not as a pre-text for the exercise of an empty ingenuity by interpreters. But this, it should be noted, is an ethical demand. It always remains possible to treat a poem, a technical manual, or my neighbour's speech in a deconstructive way. I will only treat these things as having a (relatively) determinate meaning to convey if I am engaged in a situation in which I am interested in communicating and in being communicated with. Kierke-gaard's aesthete, who is only interested in possibilities of enjoyment, and who is concerned precisely to avoid any

---

[55] Again, whether or not Derrida really thinks of himself as a sceptic (and he certainly does not have Quine's or Davidson's pretensions to scientific objectivity) is not relevant for my purposes. The effect of his thought is sceptical.

commitments, any relationships to others, was already aware of the possibility of a 'deconstructive' approach:

The whole secret lies in arbitrariness. People usually think it easy to be arbitrary, but it requires much study to succeed in being arbitrary so as not to lose oneself in it, but so as to derive satisfaction from it. One does not enjoy the immediate, but something quite different which he arbitrarily imports into it. You go to see the middle of a play, you read the third part of a book. By this means you ensure yourself a very different kind of enjoyment from that which the author has been so kind as to plan for you.[56]

2.3.3. *Wittgenstein*

Throughout his philosophical career Wittgenstein was concerned with the idea of disengagement. Not only does this lie behind the enigmatic Schopenhauerian 'solipsism' of the *Tractatus*, but it is also reflected in the whole philosophy of language advanced in that work. The first part of *Philosophical Investigations* is devoted by Wittgenstein to a critique of the assumptions underlying his earlier work; his fundamental point is that language is not the product of a disengaged mind making assertions, picturing facts to itself in propositions, but is, rather, the product of people in society, performing practical tasks and fulfilling practical needs. The idea of the self as a detached intellect fundamentally distorts our understanding of language. 'The speaking of language is part of an activity, or of a form of life.'[57] Without the practical, social—engaged—activities of embodied persons, language would not be possible at all. Even mathematics, the most abstract and purely intellectual of sign systems, is ultimately rooted in the practicalities of human life.

Saul Kripke has reminded us of the central part that the discussion of rule-following plays in the *Investigations*. Subsequently, there has been much argument as to whether Wittgenstein is proposing a form of scepticism in these sections, and, if so, what sort of answer he attempts to give to that scepticism. I think Kripke is correct to say that Wittgenstein is concerned with the possibility of a radical scepticism in which

[56] *E/O* i. 295.
[57] L. Wittgenstein, *Philosophical Investigations*, trans. G. E. M. Anscombe (Oxford, 1981), §23.

'the entire idea of meaning vanishes into thin air'.[58] However, I see Wittgenstein's response to that scepticism rather differently from Kripke—at any rate, my emphasis is different. Wittgenstein's argument, as I see it, is essentially a *reductio ad absurdum*. In the discussion of rule-following we start with an attempt to understand language from a disengaged standpoint, to see the understanding of rules as a matter of interpretation, of forming and testing hypotheses. And we are brought to realize that, if we stick with this model, we are forced to the conclusion that language is impossible, that there is no such thing as meaning. But Wittgenstein sees this as undermining not meaning, but the disengaged stance. Hence the rule-following argument reinforces his basic insight into the essentially practical and social character of language.

The main example that Wittgenstein uses in his discussion of rules is that of continuing a mathematical series, but the ability to follow a rule—to 'go on in the same way', having been shown how a word is used—is essential to all language. The trouble is that, having been given a rule, one can, with sufficient ingenuity, find an indefinite number of different interpretations of it, each of which would account for all the previous uses of the word, but then prescribe different ways of going on in the future. And which is correct? Which one really was the rule that governed the previous uses? Once such doubts have been raised, they cannot be resolved simply by stating how a rule is to be interpreted, since that interpretation itself may be variously interpreted. An infinite regress seems to open up, and meaning disappears into the void. 'This was our paradox: no course of action could be determined by a rule, because every course of action can be made out to accord with the rule.'[59]

One can ask for any rule to be explained; and one can then ask for any explanations to be explained, because there is always the possibility of different interpretations. And there is no distinctive mental buzz that would tell us when we had finally understood the correct interpretation. (Moreover, 'even supposing I had found something that happened in all those cases of under-standing—why should *it* be the understanding?'[60]) We seem to be driven towards a Derridean vision of an infinity of possible

[58] S. Kripke, *Wittgenstein on Rules and Private Languages* (Oxford, 1982), 22.
[59] Wittgenstein, *Philosophical Investigations*, §201.   [60] Ibid. §153.

interpretations, with no means of deciding between them, a semantic anarchy in which meaning disappears. But it is precisely Wittgenstein's point that it only seems this way because we have started out with a fundamental misunderstanding. There is no theoretical point at which the multiplication of further interpretations becomes impossible—the wholly disengaged intelligence can spin around for ever, never gaining any purchase on a solid ground of meaning. (As, for Kierkegaard, any conclusion that goes beyond 'sensation and immediate cognition' may theoretically be doubted.) What brings the regress to a halt is practice. Having stated his 'paradox', Wittgenstein continues:

> it can be seen that there is a misunderstanding here from the mere fact that in the course of our argument we give one interpretation after another; as if each one contented us for at least a moment, until we thought of yet another standing behind it. What this shows is that there is a way of grasping a rule which is *not* an *interpretation* but which is exhibited in what we call 'obeying the rule' and 'going against it' in actual cases.[61]

This is not a 'sceptical solution' to 'sceptical doubts', but an undermining of scepticism, based on a rejection of the presuppositions that lead to it. As a matter of practical training, we do come to agree on how to follow rules—it remains theoretically possible to raise sceptical doubts, propose alternative interpretations, but in practice we do not. 'If I have exhausted the justifications, I have reached bedrock and my spade is turned. Then I am inclined to say "This is simply what I do." '[62] 'When I obey a rule I do not choose. I obey the rule blindly.'[63] That we have at least a relative stability of meaning is due to the brute fact that people do react more or less in the same way to their linguistic training, and do then act 'blindly' instead of trying to think out interpretations of the rules. If someone adopts some eccentric alternative interpretation, he is simply corrected. 'The meaning of a word is its use in the language'[64]— that is, the way in which the language-using community as a whole does in fact use it. While an individual may suggest modifications in usage, introduce neologisms and so on, he

---

[61] Wittgenstein, *Philosophical Investigations*, §201.
[62] Ibid. §217.   [63] Ibid. §219.   [64] Ibid. §43.

cannot, from a position of disengagement, build up a language for himself from scratch. Language emerges from the practicalities of human life, and especially of human social life. If one abstracts from that to a position of disengagement, language disappears en route. This is the point that Wittgenstein is trying to make in the Private Language argument, and, in so doing, he identifies the central flaw in the epistemological tradition stemming from Descartes, and still continued—albeit in very different ways—by Derrida and Quine.

Although they reach this conclusion by quite different routes, Wittgenstein and Derrida agree that there is no absolute metaphysical guarantee for the stability of meaning. But where Derrida sees this as licensing an indefinite freedom of interpretation, Wittgenstein sees meaning as adequately grounded in human practice. ' "So you are saying that human agreement decides what is true and false?"—it is what human beings *say* that is true and false; and they agree in the *language* they use. That is not agreement in opinions, but in form of life.'[65] Many commentators have felt that this does represent a 'sceptical solution'—to regard mere human agreement as the basis of language is a second-best, something that we have to fall back on when we realize that no more metaphysically substantial guarantees are available. But this is not, I think, how Wittgenstein sees it. For him, as for Kierkegaard, metaphysics and scepticism both derive from disengagement. The disengaged stance leads not to a deeper knowledge but only to scepticism. But, rather than abandon disengagement, we may choose to embrace that scepticism. So, for Kierkegaard, scepticism can only be broken by the will, by choosing, in full knowledge that doubts can be raised, not to doubt.

Wittgenstein does not share Kierkegaard's emphasis on will. He stresses the extent to which, like it or not, we are all engaged in social and practical life, and thus unable consistently to adopt a disengaged stance. Nevertheless, he fully recognizes the extent to which our culture has been permeated by the influence of the ideal of disengagement, and his work is an attempt to combat that influence. Like Kierkegaard, Wittgenstein aims to alter our sensibilities, to turn us away from the theoretical, detached stance, and towards practical engagement. His work is

[65] Ibid. §241.

aimed not so much at providing neat chains of valid argument, which can be taken over in an essentially unconcerned way by academic successors, but at making us more aware of how strange and unnatural the disengaged stance is, to lead us to a re-engagement, to an acceptance of the limits of the human condition. 'I am by no means sure that I should prefer a continuation of my work by others to a change in the way people live which would make all these questions superfluous.'[66]

2.4. 'TRUTH IS SUBJECTIVITY'

At the heart of Kierkegaard's thinking lies the idea summed up in the dictum 'truth is subjectivity'. This has been repeatedly, and often outrageously, misinterpreted. Sometimes Kierkegaard has been accused of asserting a general epistemological relativism, according to which 'to say that a belief is true means no more than that it is held sincerely and without reservations . . .'[67] In other words: if you believe something, then it's true for you—whatever that might mean. Another commentator claims that, for Kierkegaard, 'the belief of a Hindu that Vishnu is God, the belief of a Mohammedan that Allah is God, the belief of a Nuer that *kwoth* is God—even the belief of an atheist that there is no God—are all true; providing only that in each of these beliefs an objective uncertainty is embraced with passionate intensity.'[68] Kierkegaard's dictum has also been taken up by anti-realist philosophers of religion, such as Don Cupitt, in support of their contention that talk about God must be construed as an allegorical way of talking about subjective 'spiritual' states and attitudes of human beings.

These misinterpretations mainly arise, I suspect, because the interpreters are taking for granted, when they approach Kierkegaard's text, precisely those presuppositions which he is trying to question. I am thinking of the assumption that truth—that is, knowledge of how things really are outside us—can only be reached objectively, by abstracting from our feelings, wishes,

---

[66] L. Wittgenstein, *Culture and Value*, trans. P. Winch (Oxford, 1980), 61.
[67] P. Edwards, 'Kierkegaard and the "Truth" of Christianity', in P. Edwards and A. Pap (eds.), *A Modern Introduction to Philosophy* (New York, 1973), 513–14.
[68] W. T. Jones, *Kant to Wittgenstein and Sartre* (New York, 1969), 228.

prejudices, and so forth. So if I make a statement that is explicitly based on my feelings and on a refusal to abstract from them, it cannot claim to be 'true' except as a revelation of my emotional state. In other words, the critics are taking for granted our old friend the ideal of disengagement, which is precisely what Kierkegaard is trying to criticize. What he maintains is that there are cases where the truth—knowledge of how things really are, distinct from myself—can only be obtained subjectively. By this, he does not mean an idealistic reduction of things to the knowing mind, nor is he providing a sophistical defence of wishful thinking. The point is that—in ethical and religious matters—we can only really come to know the truth through committed action that involves the whole person—the emotional, passionate nature as well as the intellect. Knowledge is gained not by disengagement from, but through a deeper immersion in, my personal existence.

As we have seen, Kierkegaard argues that there is an element of personal commitment involved in holding any substantive proposition to be true (as opposed to merely entertaining it hypothetically), for there is an element of uncertainty in any such truth-claim. Kierkegaard's main interest, though, is in ethical and religious truth. In these, too, there is the element of uncertainty, but the demand for personal commitment here is far greater, for ethics and religion are not like science and history, in which I may be very interested, but which have no essential relation to my personal life. But ethics and religion are fundamentally concerned with the way in which I live, with what I do with my life. It makes a practical difference whether I am a Muslim, a Marxist, a Nietzschean, a Buddhist, a liberal humanist. Hence to choose ethically or ethico-religiously (and this applies to the choice of action in a concrete moral dilemma as well as to an initial choice of a value-system) must involve passion—not necessarily in the sense of a display of emotional fireworks, but in the sense of a realization of the significance of the choice to me, the direction that I am choosing to give to my existence. This is quite unlike the attitude of the detached intellectual spectator. Hence Kierkegaard defines subjective truth as 'an objective uncertainty held fast in an approximation-process of the most passionate inwardness'.[69]

[69] *CUP* 182.

This is still somewhat obscure. In particular, why does Kierkegaard call the passionate commitment to an objective uncertainty 'truth'? I shall approach this question by distinguishing three successively stronger theses, each of which Kierkegaard holds, and discussing them in turn, starting with the weakest (in the sense of the least bold, the one asserting least, not in the sense of the least plausible). The first thesis is that objective thought about ethics and religion is not enough—knowledge of 'existential' truths is worthless unless one allows them to change one's life. The second thesis is that there cannot be genuine objective knowledge about ethics and religion—someone who thinks that he has understood ethics and religion objectively has simply misunderstood them. The third thesis is that 'truth' can be attributed not only to ideas, but to attitudes: not only to beliefs but to the spirit in which they are held; not only to propositions, but to human lives.

Before proceeding, I should make it clear that Kierkegaard is not—contrary to the interpretations mentioned at the beginning of this section—arguing that the 'objective' understanding of truth (a true belief is one that accords with the facts) simply does not apply to ethico-religious beliefs. In his definition of subjective truth, quoted above, Kierkegaard mentions 'objective uncertainty'. It is because it is truth—in other words, whether our beliefs correspond to reality—that is at stake and because this is uncertain, that we must choose with passion. If there was no question of a relation to reality, then there would be no cause for passion. We would just believe whatever we liked, so long as it felt good, and there would be no reason for anxiety as to whether we were right or wrong.

What Kierkegaard does insist is that it matters not only what we believe, but how we believe it. ('The objective accent falls on WHAT is said, the subjective accent on HOW it is said.'[70]) This is the first, weakest thesis. It is important not only to have true beliefs, but also to act upon them. I do not acquire any moral merit by seeing how I should behave in a situation, if I do not act upon my understanding. For a religious believer, to assent to orthodox doctrinal propositions is not at all the same thing as to have a living faith. For, as Wittgenstein (whose thinking about religion was heavily influenced by Kierkegaard) put it: 'a sound

[70] *CUP* 181.

doctrine need not *take hold* of you . . . here you need something to move you and turn you in a new direction.'[71] That we should not merely hold correct ethico-religious beliefs, but also practise them is not controversial in theory. (Though it may be hard to apply it to ourselves in practice. Kierkegaard spent most of his last years trying to show his contemporaries that they did not act in accordance with the Christian beliefs that they professed, and had to resort to extremes of stridency and abusiveness before people started to notice.) However, Kierkegaard also holds the two stronger and far more controversial theses to which I referred above.

The second thesis is that an objective, uncommitted belief in ethical and religious matters is not only inadequate, but impossible. In existential matters, a purely intellectual belief is not a real belief at all. Kierkegaard notes that, even in non-existential matters, we sometimes say that 'what is in itself true may in the mouth of such and such a person become untrue.'[72] Furthermore, we find it natural to say of someone who professes certain ethico-religious beliefs but makes no attempt to act on them (even to the extent of feeling guilty about his failings), that he 'does not really believe' what he claims to. Thought and action are, after all, closely related, and it can be argued that someone's actions reveal his intentions and beliefs and emotions more accurately than his speech, even if it is consciously sincere. This, indeed, is one of the presuppositions of the psychology of the unconscious[73] (of which Kierkegaard himself was a pioneer). It follows that we should not ascribe a belief to somebody simply on the basis of his own say-so; even if he is not being consciously hypocritical, he may be deceiving himself. One needs to see whether the person as a whole—with his whole emotional and volitional nature—believes something, or whether, so to speak, it is only his conscious mind that so believes.

If we are justified in speaking of unconscious beliefs, which we ascribe to people on the basis of their actions, there seems to be no prima-facie objection to assessing these beliefs for their

[71] Wittgenstein, *Culture and Value*, 53. [72] *CUP* 181.
[73] Psychologists have held that there are other ways of exploring the unconscious, of course; most notably, through dreams. But the apparently arbitrary (and sometimes fantastic) nature of Freudian and Jungian dream-interpretation does little to convince the sceptic of the value of this method.

truth or falsity. This means that—given sufficiently strong evidence—we could reasonably describe somebody as having certain true (or false) beliefs even if this contradicted his own sincere account of what he believed. This is part of what I have described as Kierkegaard's third and strongest thesis—that a life may be true even though its consciousness is false (or vice versa). I will say more about this later, but at the moment I am concerned to defend the second, and weaker, thesis, which is a negative one: that there cannot be a wholly objective, purely intellectual belief in ethico-religious matters. For this purpose, I need only to argue that the evidence of someone's behaviour can negate a claim to believe something, leaving on one side the question of whether such evidence alone is enough to justify an ascription of belief. Even if the relevant behaviour is not a sufficient condition for ascribing belief, it is, I think, at least a necessary condition. If I claim to hold certain beliefs about the way in which one should live, but make no effort whatsoever to live as those beliefs prescribe, what is the content of my claim to believe?

I have been speaking of 'behavioural' evidence, but this needs to be qualified. Someone may have genuine ethical principles but still act badly; a sincere religious believer may still be a great sinner. The genuineness of their beliefs would become apparent in their feelings of guilt, remorse, and repentance. But although such feelings would normally have some impact on the penitent's behaviour, I am certainly not suggesting that they can be defined in behaviouristic terms. Whether someone is a hypocrite or a sincere but weak-willed believer may not be apparent to an observer of his behaviour. Hence the genuineness of someone's beliefs may be a matter of what Kierkegaard calls 'hidden inwardness'. (Though it is worth noting that, in his later works, he came to repudiate the idea of hidden inwardness, and to insist that belief finds expression in actions.) Moreover, actions are frequently ambiguous, open to various possible interpretations. My thesis is not, therefore, a behaviouristic one; it is intended to contrast an attitude of the whole person—the affective and emotional nature that will normally find expression in action—with a purely intellectual assent to propositions.

Why can objective reasoning not produce ethical or religious knowledge? The short answer is that such knowledge is essentially concerned with the individual's search for meaning and fulfilment in his life. Ethics, for Kierkegaard—as I will show in detail in the next chapter—is not about social regulations, nor is it about obedience to Kantian-style absolute moral precepts. It is about each individual's search for what will give meaning to his life. Now, Kierkegaard's argument is not that we must each find—or even create—our own values for ourselves. The ethical, as he says, is the universal,[74] and involves a commitment to social relationships such as work, marriage and family life. Beyond the ethical, the religious is concerned with the individual's relationship to God. Kierkegaard's ethics is therefore teleological, in that it is concerned to point towards the good life for man, how human happiness and fulfilment can be found. But one cannot objectively specify the conditions for human flourishing, as a botanist may specify the conditions under which a species of plant may flourish. This is not to say that objective reasoning plays no part in ethics—one may, for instance, argue that man is a social animal, and therefore needs a society in which to flourish, in much the same way as a zoologist might argue about some other species—but, to have any force, such arguments must pass though subjectivity. That is, ethics has ultimately to base itself on people's own perceptions of their needs. An ethical argument is valid in so far as it articulates an individual's— maybe initially inchoate or unconscious—sense of need, his hunger for meaning, fulfilment. The fundamental question in ethics is: How shall I live? But this is a question that is necessarily asked from the first personal standpoint, that is, from the standpoint not of an abstract subject, but of a real individual person, with his own particular background, psycho-logical make-up, and inclinations. It is from this concrete individuality that abstract thought tries to abstract in order to think objectively. But the primary ethical question—how shall I live?—can only be asked meaningfully by a real, concrete individual. An 'objective' approach to ethics, therefore, neces-sarily misses the point. This is why Kierkegaard's major work on ethics takes the form not of an objective treatise, but of letters written by one imaginary character to another.

As I shall show in the next chapter, this feature of ethical thought does not preclude rigorous and even quite generalized

---

[74] Cf. *FT* 54, 68, 82.

argumentation. But such arguments have a purely 'hypothetical' character until I apply them to the facts of my own life. As we have seen, Kierkegaard argues that this is, to some extent, true of all knowledge. I can develop theories, elaborate conceptual possibilities, but the question of truth or falsity arises only when I try to apply them to reality. This is also true of ethical theories; but the application in this case consists in the effort to live by them. A scientific theory may be tested quite objectively, but the test of an ethical theory lies precisely within human subjectivity. Ultimately, the only ground that I may have for believing in the truth of an ethical theory is that I have found fulfilment as a result of living in a way that it commends; or that I have experienced a lack of fulfilment as a result of living in a way that is significantly different. Hence Kierkegaard's dialectic of the 'stages on life's way'; the felt inadequacy of living at one stage is what forces one on to the next. Kierkegaard is not arguing that one should experiment with every possible way of life (though he was fascinated by the Carpocratian sect, which held that salvation was found by living through all the possibilities for both good and evil[75]). One can gain an understanding of different ways of life, and their attractions and weaknesses, without actually living in these ways oneself. This understanding may be gained through personal contact or through literature (this was precisely the point of Kierkegaard's own more literary writings—to make different ways of life vivid to the imagination). But not through objective treatises, for what they leave out in order to be objective is precisely what is essential—the subjective element.

Kierkegaard's attack on objectivism is most fully developed in his account of religious belief. He notes two possible approaches to religious faith: that of 'the one who seeks the true God objectively, and pursues the approximate truth of the God-idea'; and that of 'one who, driven by the infinite passion of his need of God, feels an infinite concern for his own relationship to God in truth'.[76] The former 'enters upon the entire approximation-process by which it is proposed to bring God to light objectively. But this is in all eternity impossible, because God is a subject, and therefore exists only for subjectivity in inwardness.'[77]

---

[75] Cf. e.g. *CA* 103.   [76] *CUP* 179.   [77] Ibid. 178.

Kierkegaard is not saying here that God's existence is somehow relative to, or dependent on, the faith of His believers, but that God, as a subject, can only be known through another subject's relation to Him. Attempts to know God objectively miss the living God by turning Him into an object or a purely conceptual being.

The various traditional attempts to prove God's existence by objective reasoning are given a sceptical treatment by Kierkegaard in chapter 3 of the *Fragments*. Given his general hostility to efforts to blur the distinction between thought and existence, he naturally rejects the 'ontological argument', which seeks to demonstrate that God's real existence follows from the very concept of God. But he also rejects the 'teleological' argument, which takes the order of nature as a proof of God. 'I contemplate the order of nature in the hope of finding God, and I see omnipotence and wisdom; but I also see much else that disturbs my mind and excites anxiety. The sum of all this is an objective uncertainty.'[78] Kierkegaard does not simply dismiss the traditional proofs of God as worthless, however, for they testify to a 'passion of the understanding',[79] a natural inclination of the human mind to reach out for a complete explanation of things, for complete comprehension. In this passion the reason comes up against the limit of understanding, beyond which it can think no further.

At this point Kierkegaard seems to have been influenced by Kant's doctrine of the Transcendental Ideas, particularly the idea of God, as limit-concepts. We can affirm the idea of God— indeed, we are naturally led to do so by the desire of the reason for a completeness of understanding that can rest in the idea of a 'first and final cause'—but, since this lies beyond the limits of possible experience, we cannot think anything definite in connection with this idea, nor even have a rational proof that anything real corresponds to it. Kant writes that 'Natural theology is such a concept at the boundary of human reason, being constrained to look beyond this boundary to the Idea of a Supreme Being', but is unable to 'determine anything relative to this pure creature of the understanding'.[80] For Kierkegaard, too,

---

[78] Ibid. 182.   [79] *PhF* 44.
[80] I. Kant, *Prolegomena to Any Future Metaphysics*, trans. P. Carus (La Salle, Ill., n.d.), §59, p. 134.

it is natural for a thinker to come to ask about the meaning and cause of the world as a whole—a 'limited whole', apt to be squeezed into a ball, and rolled towards the overwhelming question of its origin and purpose. The trouble is that, although we can ask the question, we cannot answer it.

Objective thought has now broken down. The enigmatic 'unknown god' to which reason has brought us is unsatisfying; we try to give this blank idea some content by drawing on all the resources of our imagination, hence the multiplicity of strange and wonderful religious beliefs. But 'at the very bottom of devoutness there madly lurks the capricious arbitrariness that knows it itself has produced the god.'[81] Objective reasoning about religion can, if it is honest, only reach agnostic conclusions. In book 1 of the *Postscript* Kierkegaard demolishes the idea that the historical study of a historical religion such as Christianity can produce any conclusion as to whether or not it is true religion. However much we may come to know about some past event, it still takes a leap of faith to acknowledge that event as a revelation from God. Accordingly, someone who claims that he has arrived at religious belief through a process of objective reasoning is just wrong—his reasoning has gone astray somewhere. Furthermore, he will be under the false impression that what he believes is objectively certain, or at least probable, which it is not. This means that he is under a serious misapprehension; he has, to some extent, failed to understand what he thought he believed—for he thought it was objectively reasonable, and it is not.

All that objective reasoning can do in religion is to arrive at the blank, indeterminate, and dubiously applicable notion of some unknowable reality beyond the limits of the empirical world. If we wish to arrive at any substantive religious beliefs, these can only come through subjectivity, through the attitude of one who is 'driven by the infinite passion of his need of God'.[82] Kierkegaard would, of course, wish to distinguish this from the 'capricious arbitrariness' that invents its own conceptions of deity. Ultimately, he would answer that it is only out of the depth of my need for God that I can grasp what is not a human conception at all, but God's self-revelation. But what he principally insists on in the *Postscript* is that, by the quality of my

[81] *PhF* 45.   [82] *CUP* 179.

faith—even if it is directed to a false or inadequate or arbitrary concept of God, I may still in fact relate to the true God. But this takes us on to Kierkegaard's third thesis, which concerns the nature of subjective truth.

According to Kierkegaard, we can ascribe truth and falsity not just to beliefs and propositions, but to the spirit in which they are held. And, ultimately, this means that we can speak of a person, a human life, being true or being 'in the truth'. The only sense that objective thinking will make of such a claim is that someone is in the truth if what he believes is, in fact, true. But 'when the question of truth is raised subjectively, reflection is directed subjectively to the nature of the individual's relationship; if only the mode of this relationship is in the truth, the individual is in the truth, even if he should happen to be thus related to what is not true.'[83] It is worth pointing out again that what Kierkegaard is concerned with here is 'essential', that is, ethico-religious knowledge, the only knowledge that 'has an essential relationship to the existence of the knower'.[84] This makes it possible to raise the question of whether a life is true. To the reality of nature being such and such, there may correspond a true scientific theory; to the reality of an ethical demand, there corresponds, primarily, a life that is lived in a certain way. An understanding of nature is expressed in the utterance of true sentences;[85] an understanding of ethics and religion is expressed in a way of life.

As I have pointed out above, Kierkegaard does not mean that the issue of whether ethico-religious statements or propositions are true simply becomes irrelevant. What he does point to is that someone's consciously formulated beliefs may be true, while his life is false, and vice versa. And if the two collide, it is the lived truth that matters. 'Precisely as important as the truth, and if one of the two is to be emphasised, still more important, is the manner in which the truth is accepted. It would help very little if one persuaded millions of men to accept the truth, if precisely by the method of their acceptance, they were transferred into error.'[86] On the other hand, someone may be living 'in the

[83] Ibid. 178. [84] Ibid. 177.
[85] One might well want to argue for a more pragmatic, more experimental, less purely representational account of science than this. Even scientific thinking may need to be understood as essentially related to human practice—though not necessarily to ethical practice. [86] *CUP* 221.

truth', even if his conscious beliefs are all wrong. Someone may act rightly, even though his ethical beliefs are confused or false or downright evil.[87] We would normally say that he was a better person than one who had the right beliefs but behaved badly. Kierkegaard would go further, and say that it was the first person who was closer to the truth. For ethics is about how to act, and ethical truth is manifested primarily in right action.

Kierkegaard also applies this perspective to religion.

If one who lives in the midst of Christendom goes up to the house of God, the house of the true God, with the true conception of God in his knowledge and prays, but prays in a false spirit; and one who lives in an idolatrous community prays with the entire passion of the infinite, although his eyes rest on the image of an idol; where is there most truth? The one prays in truth to God, though he worships an idol; the other prays falsely to the true God, and hence worships in fact an idol.[88]

One should note how different this is from the caricature interpretation of Kierkegaard, according to which all sincerely held beliefs are equally true. Kierkegaard is assuming that Christianity is true and the idolater's beliefs are false; but his interest is in the truth or falsity of the two worshippers' attitudes. The idolater's beliefs are wrong, but his state of mind is one of devotion, humility, need for God—and, because of this, he does succeed in relating to the true God, despite the inadequacy of his concept of God. This outlook seems to have been accepted by many modern theologians. In the last few centuries the mainstream Christian Churches have acquired a welcome squeamishness about asserting the damnation of all those outside their own communion; hence the acceptance that someone may, by his way of life, acquire a relation to God, despite the inadequacy, or even lack, of his conscious belief in God. Again we see that, for Kierkegaard, there is a kind of knowledge that is distinct from, and more important than, conscious, intellectual knowledge, but which can be traced in the attitudes and actions of the knower.

---

[87] A good literary example is Huckleberry Finn's decision to help the escape of a slave, despite his sincerely held 'moral' belief that slaves are property and should therefore be returned to their owners. There is an interesting discussion of this, and some other cases, in J. Bennett, 'The Conscience of Huckleberry Finn', *Philosophy*, 1974.   [88] *CUP* 179–80.

This may still be controversial. Some philosophers would want to say: 'Very well. The objective approach to ethico-religious truth is misconceived. It is important not just to have correct beliefs, but to act on them, and someone who acts rightly but has false beliefs may be morally better and closer to God than someone who has true beliefs but fails to act on them. But why should we talk about subjective "truth" in this connection? How can a mood or an attitude be true? For truth is a property of propositions or beliefs.' But if we ascribe truth to beliefs, need these necessarily be conscious, intellectually formulated beliefs? I have already argued that there is sense in speaking of unconscious beliefs, expressed in someone's actions and emotions, rather than in intellectualized formulations. And why should we not consider these in terms of truth or falsity?

The concept of truth is intimately associated with that of reality. A true proposition is one that describes how things really are.[89] But to confine the concept of truth to propositional truth is a piece of arbitrary semantic legislation. One need not quarrel too loudly over a word, but when Kierkegaard talks about the truth of a life, he is not abusing language or misusing the concept of truth; he is extending that concept in a legitimate way by drawing our attention to real analogies that philosophers have tended to overlook. Truth is a relatedness to reality, an openness to it, which enables reality to become manifest, to find expression. A proposition may do this, but there is no need to restrict our attention to propositions. A work of art may be truthful—it may express or focus reality for us; this is the case, indeed, with music, which so often gives us the sense of expressing deep truths which are quite impossible to translate into propositions.

Kierkegaard's point is that a human life, or certain moments within it, may also legitimately be described as true (or false). In ethico-religious terms, a life is true if it is open to, and therefore able to make manifest, the reality of ethical demands, the reality

---

[89] I am aware of the difficulties that arise when one tries to formalize this simple intuition as a 'correspondence theory of truth'. For one thing, the 'facts' to which true propositions are supposed to correspond can only be identified by repeating the propositions. But my remark is intended simply to state the truism; it is not a philosophical theory aiming to explain the truism. 'The door is open' is true if the door is open—and that depends on the position of the door, rather than on anything about language.

of God.[90] The life of a saint may express religious truths far more profoundly than any proposition can; an action may reveal ethical realities far more clearly and fully than any amount of moralizing exhortation. Conversely, sin and evil have been understood in several traditions, both religious and secular, as forms of falsehood, blindness, false consciousness. The Socratic definition of wrongdoing as ignorance is certainly naïve, if taken in the sense of a failure to understand the definitions of moral concepts,[91] but, in an existential rather than an intellectual sense, wrongdoing or sin are states in which we are cut off from reality. In Iris Murdoch's words, we reach a state in which our consciousness is not 'a transparent glass through which [we] view the world, but a cloud of more or less fantastic reverie designed to protect the psyche from pain'.[92] There is a revealing idiom: we sometimes say of somebody that he is 'living a lie'. In a sense, all wrongdoing is living a lie; and goodness is living a truth.

Fundamentally, what Kierkegaard is reminding us of is that we do not relate to the world primarily as detached rational observers, but as agents and as emotional beings. Hence Kierkegaard studies such moods as anxiety, irony, and despair as profoundly revelatory of the reality of human existence and of the nature of the world in which we live. Our emotions are not simply factors that tend to cloud or confuse the intellect; they are ways in which we relate to the world, and may be more reliable guides to it than the intellect at times. If I see someone in pain, feel compassion for him, and attempt to help, why should I not treat my feeling as revealing to me aspects of reality (his actual experience of pain and need; our common humanity; the ethical demand that is made on me) that would simply be missed or inadequately understood by a purely rational analysis of his physical or even psychological condition? In which case, why should it not be legitimate to speak about the truth of my emotion? The exclusively intellectualist interpretation of truth is a prejudice that has bedevilled religious, ethical, and aesthetic

[90] Cf. John 14: 6: 'I am the way, the truth, and the life'. Stephen Evans suggests that Kierkegaard may have had this text in mind when formulating his conception of subjective truth.

[91] Kierkegaard has an interesting discussion of the Socratic definition in *SUD* 87–96.

[92] I. Murdoch, *The Sovereignty of Good* (London, 1970), 78–9.

thinking. Kierkegaard's teaching that 'truth is subjectivity' is a protest against that prejudice. It is therefore precisely the opposite of what it is supposed to be by the reductive critics quoted at the beginning of this section. Kierkegaard is not saying that there is no truth, it is all subjective; but, rather, what is revealed through subjectivity is truth, is the real nature of things.

3

THE ETHICAL

In this chapter I shall discuss the first main transition or leap that is required for the progress through Kierkegaard's stages of life, that from the aesthetic to the ethical. This is presented mainly in *Either/Or*. Many moral philosophers have liked to set up a figure called the amoralist. He plays a similar role to his cousin, the sceptic, in epistemology, in that if arguments can be found that will win him over to accepting morality (or knowledge), then the rational basis of morality (or knowledge) will have been triumphantly demonstrated. The amoralist is usually a bit of a straw man, a rather colourless place-holder for a position of theoretical interest. It is part of Kierkegaard's achievement, in trying to make philosophy 'existential', that in *Either/Or* he presents us with an extremely vivid literary portrayal of an amoralist, in the person of young 'A', the aesthete. (The vividness of the characterization is no doubt partly due to the fact that *Either/Or* is, amongst other things, a Portrait of the Artist as a Young Man.) Though he may find it amusing now and again to play around with ethical categories, 'A' has no serious use for them at all; he does not see his own life in moral terms. Kierkegaard shows us what one kind of amoralist may actually look like, how he understands his life, and therefore raises the question of what arguments would actually convince a living person of this sort to enter the realm of morality. Neat-looking neo-Kantian arguments that appear convincing in the abstract, in a philosopher's study, may seem a little hollow if we imagine them being read with 'A' 's mocking eyes. Accordingly, in the second volume of *Either/Or* Kierkegaard presents not a formal ethical treatise, addressed to the reasoning powers of any rational agent, but personal letters of advice sent to 'A' by a friend. In what follows, I shall be providing a rational reconstruction of their argument, but, inevitably, the direct literary flavour that is a central part of Kierkegaard's philosophical method will be lost. I can only repeat my earlier apology for this—unavoidable—inadequacy, and carry on philosophically.

Schematically, then, the argument that Judge William, Kierkegaard's spokesman for the ethical, brings against 'A' is as follows:

1. One can only avoid the necessity of judging one's life in moral terms by evading long-term commitments.
2. But to live such a life is to be in despair; for a life without commitments is one without purpose, and hence is one that makes it impossible to develop a coherent personal identity.
3. Therefore, personal fulfilment and the avoidance of despair can only be found by taking on such commitments and by accepting the moral judgements that one's performance in these roles entails.

I will now examine this line of argument in more detail.

The aesthete may reasonably be described as someone who has awoken to an awareness of possibility. Intellectually, he is a doubter; not an academic doubter who practises Cartesian methodology as a first step on the way to building up a System, but someone more akin to a Greek sceptic, who, in the face of the difficulties that can be found with virtually any belief, is unable to commit himself to any of them. Kierkegaard liked to identify this tendency to doubt with the figure of Faust, and certainly saw himself as strongly tempted to abandon himself to such Faustian scepticism: 'My doubt is terrible.—Nothing can withstand it.—It is a cursed hunger and I can swallow up every argument, every consolation, and sedative.—I rush at 10,000 miles a second through every obstacle.'[1]

Such scepticism is existential. The aesthetic doubter is aware of the indefinite range of possibilities open to him, of how many and how various are the possible answers to the question: How should I live? But this perception has a paralysing effect. Being able imaginatively to identify with a great variety of possible attitudes or outlooks, he becomes incapable of committing himself to any one in particular. Alternatives are too vividly present to him, his moods rapidly changeable, and his actions

[1] Dru, 5494.

are determined by his moods, by inclination, by whatever appeals most powerfully to his imagination at any given time. Hence he has no constancy of purpose. He has recognized that, in matters of practical choice especially, one can, with a bit of ingenuity, find good reasons for all sorts of different alternatives. Whereas the ethicist—and, even more, the religious believer—concludes from this that one must simply launch out in one of the possible directions, commit oneself to it, make the leap of faith, the aesthete concludes from the bankruptcy of reason in existential matters that decisive choice is itself an absurdity; accordingly, he chooses to do whatever it is that happens to fit in with his mood at the time.

Ask whatever questions you please, but do not ask me for reasons. A young woman may be forgiven for not being able to give reasons, since they say she lives in her feelings. Not so with me. I generally have so many reasons, and most often such mutually contradictory reasons, that for this reason it is impossible for me to give reasons.[2]

Whereas the immediate aesthete, such as the 'young woman' about whom Kierkegaard generalizes, but also the Don Juan character, just acts on impulse, the reflective aesthete either fails to act at all because he reflects too much, or he reflects until he is sick of reflection; and then just acts on impulse anyway. But even such action is lacking in spontaneity—and his imaginative powers have given him an unusually wide repertoire of impulses and desires. 'No pregnant woman can have stronger or more impatient desires than I. These desires concern sometimes the most trivial things, sometimes the most exalted, but they are equally imbued with the soul's momentary passion.'[3]

Refusing to judge his life in ethical terms, the aesthete is concerned with enjoying himself. Thus the great threat is boredom. The only piece of general aesthetic theorizing that Kierkegaard gives us is the short essay 'The Rotation Method' in *Either/Or*. Here a variety of strategies for escaping boredom are recommended. What is notable is the way in which the individual is regarded as wholly isolated; seeing himself as distinct from society and only externally related to others, he sets out to discover how he can succeed in leading an enjoyable

---

[2] *E/O* i. 25.   [3] Ibid. 26.

life. 'People talk so much about man being a social animal; at bottom, he is a beast of prey, and the evidence for this is not confined to the shape of his teeth. All this talk about society and the social is partly inherited hyprocrisy, partly calculated cunning.'[4] 'A' goes on to advise us that by cultivating 'the art of remembering and forgetting', we can 'insure against sticking fast in some relationship of life, and make possible the realisation of a complete freedom'.[5] Accordingly, he warns against friendship, against marriage, and against accepting 'appointment to an offical position'.[6] This does not mean that one should be inactive, that one's life should be 'deprived of the erotic element', or that 'one should abstain from social contacts'. On the contrary, all these things can be sources of great entertainment and enjoyment; the point is that one must avoid commitment—one must be able to 'sheer off at will' from any relationship. If not, then one is trapped. 'When you are one of several, then you have lost your freedom; you cannot send for your travelling boots whenever you wish, you cannot move aimlessly about in the world.'[7]

The greatest danger, then, is to get involved in an 'I–Thou' relationship.[8] 'A' also warns against work, which is all very well for him, since (like Kierkegaard) he has a private income. Less fortunate aesthetes must presumably work for their living, while maintaining an ironic distance from that work. (They must not, that is, see the job that they do as conferring any stable identity on them; they make no inner commitment to it, are essentially unconcerned with it and with whether or not they are judged to be good or bad at it, although they are committed to work by external circumstances.) It is this refusal to get involved, to make long-term commitments, that makes the aesthete an amoralist. This is a vital point. For Kierkegaard, morality is a product of commitment to roles and relationships. It is quite frequently claimed that Kierkegaard's ethics is largely Kantian, but this seems to me about as radical an error as it is possible to make in the interpretation of Kierkegaard. Nowhere does he say anything about morality being a condition of

---

[4] Ibid. 284.   [5] Ibid. 291.   [6] Ibid. 294.   [7] Ibid. 293.
[8] I mean by this roughly the same as Buber; the point is that such a relationship involves commitment and a concern for the other person in his/her own right, rather than simply as far as he/she is amusing or useful to oneself.

rationally consistent action; his mockery of the 'pure subject', and his insistence on the need for passionate existential choice are diametrically opposed to the Kantian idea that morality can be proved to be a condition of action for any rational agent. I will say more later about Kierkegaard's attitude to Kant's ethics; for the moment I can simply point to the fact that Judge William does not argue that 'A' should adopt rationally universalizable maxims, but insists, rather, that he commit himself to social roles and personal relationships. It is this sort of commitment that is central to ethics as Kierkegaard understands it, and as Judge William advocates it.

In *Either/Or* morality is presented as something that arises with the willingness to make long-term commitments, to accept social roles, and, by so doing, to accept the standards of evaluation that go with them. In a given society there are fairly clear criteria as to what constitutes a good judge, husband, father, citizen, etc.—there is no gap to be bridged between 'fact' and 'value'. By accepting the role of husband or judge within a society, one accepts the standards of evaluation that go with those roles. As Bernard Williams puts it: 'various sorts of title and rôle can conceptually carry with them broad standards of assessment of people under those titles, as the descriptions of artifacts can carry standards of assessment of those artifacts.'[9]

The problem is, however (I shall develop this point later on), that a social morality of this type, an ethics of 'my station and its duties', has become intensely problematical in the modern world, since the rise of self-conscious individualism has opened a gulf between the individual and the roles that he plays. The passage that I quoted from Bernard Williams above continues: 'While the standards can be in this way logically welded to the title, the title is not logically welded to the man.'[10] In many communities titles have been—and are—welded to people; not logically, but sociologically. But in our type of society, where the disengaged ideal flourishes, there is instead a widespread sense of a lack of any weld joining individuals more than just contingently to their social roles. Even Kierkegaard's aesthetes cannot simply drop out of society altogether, especially if they

[9] B. Williams, *Morality: An Introduction to Ethics* (Cambridge, 1976), 66.
[10] Ibid.

have no private incomes and so have to work for their livings. The aesthete cannot wholly avoid occupying social roles, but he will refuse to admit that they do anything to define him as a person. To take one of Bernard Williams's examples: a reluctant bank clerk who hates banking cannot deny that he is a bank clerk, but 'he does not, in any important sense, think of himself as a bank clerk'.[11] He needs the money that he earns, of course, so he wants to avoid getting sacked, and may even try to win promotion, but he does not care beyond that whether or not he does his job well. If he is a bad bank clerk, that does not bother him—he does not consider this to be a judgement on him *qua* person, only *qua* bank clerk, and he has no interest in being good at that.

The ethicist is different, in that he chooses to accept social roles, and therefore chooses to accept that the institutionally defined criteria of good and bad performance of these roles are relevant to him. In an 'important sense', Kierkegaard's Judge William does see himself *as* a citizen, *as* a judge, and *as* a husband and father. If, by the objective criteria of the society in which he lives, he is bad at being those things, this is not a criticism that he can laugh off, as the bank clerk could the criticism of his banking abilities; such criticism goes to the heart. It does so because he is judged and found wanting not simply in something that he is, but in what he is—what he has chosen to be. The reflective ethicist is aware that the social order in which he lives is not immutable; he knows that he can refuse to adopt social positions, or that, even if he does, he can take up an ironically distanced attitude towards them. But he chooses not to. He chooses to commit himself to a certain relationship, to playing a certain part in a social organization. More generally, he chooses broadly to accept the social conventions governing the distinctions between good and evil behaviour. Because he has made these choices, the ethicist has consciously taken himself into a sphere of life where he must apply to himself the predicates 'good' and 'evil', where he must judge himself in moral terms, according to the commonly accepted criteria. 'What is it, then, that I distinguish in my either/or? Is it good and evil? No,

---

[11] Ibid. 69.

I would only bring you up to the point where the choice between the evil and the good acquires significance for you.'[12] Again:

My either/or does not in the first instance denote the choice between good and evil; it denotes the choice whereby one chooses good *and* evil/ or excludes them. Here the question is under what determinants one would contemplate the whole of existence, and would himself live . . . for the aesthetical is not the evil but neutrality . . . it is, therefore, not so much a question of choosing between willing the good *or* the evil as of choosing to will, but by this in turn the good and the evil are posited.[13]

How is it that good and evil are 'posited' by the act of willing? By 'choosing to will', Kierkegaard refers to one's becoming willing to make some serious and long-term commitment, such as marriage, starting a career, or—though this is something beyond the limits of the Judge's horizons—a religious conversion. So long as one is able to drift without essentially committing oneself to anything or anyone, the categories of good and evil do not arise. For only by committing oneself to some project can one make the judgement that one is doing well or badly in it. A man who marries may be a bad husband, but, in so far as he takes his marriage seriously, his recognition of the fact that he is a bad husband must make him feel guilt, remorse, regret. Because he has made a commitment to a long-term relationship, and one that is of importance to him, he cannot simply shrug off the complaint that he is a bad husband, in the fashion of the reluctant bank clerk; because he is committed to being a husband, the judgement that he is a bad one is a judgement on him as a man. To fail in a project to which one has made an essential commitment is to fail—in part, anyway—as a human being.

To choose to take on a long-term commitment to a project, to choose to see oneself as a judge, a citizen of the *polis*, a member of the trade union, a husband, a mother, or whatever, is to accept that one may be judged in terms of the criteria of performance that attach to these roles. It is, to recall Bernard Williams's remark, to choose to 'weld' to oneself a 'title' that carries the 'standards of assessment' with it. It is true that there is no initial 'logical' weld of person to title; the connection was once a social fact—titles and positions were clamped around a person in virtue of his birth and upbringing—and must now be brought about by an act of existential choice.

When Judge William stresses the importance of choice, however, he does not in the first place mean the choice of a career, the decision to marry, etc.—in other words, a specific, particular choice. He refers, rather, to what he regards as a precondition of making such specific choices with the seriousness that they deserve: 'But what is it I choose? Is it this thing or that? No, for I choose absolutely, and the absoluteness of my choice is expressed precisely by the fact that I have not chosen to choose this or that. I choose the absolute. And what is the absolute? It is I myself in my eternal validity.'[14] But what is it to choose oneself in this way? The answer is that it is to choose to become a self. For Kierkegaard, the self is not a—Cartesian or other—substance that is simply given; it is something that must be achieved. Each individual human being has a potentiality for selfhood, but to realize this potential, to become a self, is, Kierkegaard argues, a strenuous task. Indeed, it is *the* ethical or ethico-religous task; it is the self that is developed by one who passes through the various stages of life. A human being is a body, a physical organism, also a set of psychological dispositions and capacities. The ethical task is to integrate the various aspects of human existence into a stable and coherent personality. This is what the aesthete lacks; his life falls apart into a series of disconnected moments; his various aptitudes and abilities may find separate expression, but they are not integrated with each other: 'You are hovering above yourself, and what you behold beneath you is a mutliplicity of moods and situations, which you employ to find interesting contacts with life.'[15]

The ethicist, on the contrary, chooses to be a self, chooses to integrate his various capacities, to acquire a stability and constancy of disposition. Hence Judge William's insistence that an ethical life does not exclude the aesthetic factor, and, indeed, that it permits its development more fully than a wholly aesthetic way of life does. Hence, too, his condemnation not only of simple hedonism for ignoring man's spiritual capacities and needs, but also of mystical religiosity for its contemptuous attitude to physical, bodily life.[16] The process of existential

---

[14] Ibid. 218.   [15] Ibid. 203.   [16] Ibid. 245–55.

choice is in radical opposition to what I have called disengagement. In choosing myself, I accept myself precisely as I am; I do not try to stand back from the complexities of my empirical self, or to take refuge in the idea of myself as pure subject, only rather contingently related to my psycho-physical personality.

> The man we are speaking of discovers now that the self he chooses contains an endless multiplicity, insomuch as it has a history, a history in which he acknowledges identity with himself . . . in this history he stands in relation to other individuals of the race, and to the race as a whole, and this history contains something painful, and yet he is the man he is only in consequence of this history.[17]

In ethical choice, I do not reject all that has gone before in order to make a fresh start; on the contrary, I take responsibility for what I am, for all the complexity of my personality, all the conflicting elements in it, and all the guilt that I have acquired; I choose myself in the sense that I choose to make of this raw material a coherent, stable, disciplined self. This is my personal ethical task. In this connection, the Judge likes to use the word 'repentance', although, as James Collins points out, what he seems to mean by it is 'more an honest recognition of the individual in his concrete nature than a religious sorrow over sinfulness'.[18] In accepting that I am what my culture and society, my own past, my upbringing and my genetic inheritance have made me, I learn to look on myself not as a pure subject, able to embrace any possibility whatsoever, but as a finite and limited human being. From the extreme point of disengaged individualism, I return to solidarity with my society, my culture, my family, my own empirical self, and its past. I recognize that what I am now is the outcome of what I have been, and so take responsibility for my past, accept my life as a developing unity across time rather than a mere succession of unconnected, aesthetic moments.

In insisting that I choose myself within my specific historical situation, as a particular person not as a 'pure self', Judge William insists that I must choose myself as part of my community.

---

[17] *E/O* ii. 220.
[18] J. Collins, *The Mind of Kierkegaard* (Princeton, NJ, 1983), 84–5.

He who has ethically chosen and found himself possesses himself as he is determined in his whole concretion. He has himself, then, as an individual who has these talents, these passions, these inclinations, these habits, who is under these influences . . . Here, then, he has himself as a task, in such a sort that the task is principally to order, cultivate, temper, enkindle, repress, in short to bring about a proportionality in the soul, a harmony, which is the fruit of the personal virtues . . . But although he himself is his aim . . . the self which is the aim is not an abstract self, which fits in everywhere and hence nowhere, but a concrete self which stands in reciprocal relations with these surroundings, these conditions of life, this natural order. This self which is the aim is not merely a personal self, but a social, a civic self. He has, then, himself as a task for an activity wherewith as this definite personality, he takes a hand in the affairs of life.[19]

We have here, then, a distinction between personal and civic virtues. The former make for a harmonious, unified self, the latter for a harmonious fitting of each individual into the wider society of which he is a part. Someone who cultivates only the personal virtues, Judge William argues,[20] has chosen himself only abstractly; he refuses to acknowledge that he is in fact a product of a specific society and can find fulfilment only in relation to that society. The disengaged self is the abstract self, and the abstract self is—precisely—an abstraction, unreal in itself. Judge William's point is not that the individual should abandon himself to social norms imposed by external force, but that self-fulfilment is the fulfilment of a social self; not a self that is somehow social in the abstract, but which is part of—and has been shaped by—a particular society. In fact, the Judge spends less time discussing civic duty than he does discussing personal relationships—especially, of course, marriage. In the *Stages on Life's Way* he goes so far as to declare: 'Marriage I regard then as the highest *telos* of individual life.'[21] Both here and in *Either/Or* the Judge spends a great deal of time trying to show that the long-term commitment of marriage is compatible with the spontaneity of sexual love. The point being made is twofold. First, the ethical individual imposes the disciplines of commitment upon the immediacy of his desires—and, by so doing, gains

[19] *E/O* ii. 266–7.
[20] Ibid. 245. This point, of course, is very Hegelian; but so, indeed, is the Judge's whole argument.   [21] *SLW* 101.

even in aesthetic terms. And, secondly, the individual cannot find fulfilment by remaining simply an individual, but only in relationship to another. This view is the precise opposite to that expressed by 'A' in 'The Rotation Method'.

But is this all that *Either/Or* offers us? Is it just a contrast of two radically opposed and incompatible views of life, which demands that we choose between them, but which provides no criteria for making such a choice? This is a widespread view. MacIntyre, for one, writes: 'the doctrine of *'Enten-Eller'* is plainly to the effect that the principles which depict the ethical way of life are to be adopted *for no reason*, but for a choice that lies beyond reasons, just because it is the choice of what is to count for us as a reason.'[22] Yet this ignores the fact that Judge William is constantly arguing; he is not just giving portraits of the ethical life, he is trying to persuade 'A' to adopt it, and he gives reasons why 'A' should do so. True, Kierkegaard does not tell us whether these arguments were effective or not, and no umpire appears to decide between 'A' and 'B'. But this just means that the reader must make up his own mind about the arguments, as they are presented. In real life there is no umpire to tell you who is correct; and, if there were, he would have no more authority than 'B' has already.

The Judge's arguments are powerful, though, because they are concerned with what 'A'—or anyone else—is interested in attaining: happiness, well-being, *eudaimonia*. The argument is that the aesthetic life is a succession of moments of brilliance and enjoyment, but that these have no connection with one another; there is no sequence or continuity in the aesthete's life. When the pleasure of the moment is past, it is simply past, as though it had never been; nothing has been achieved. Boredom supervenes, and can only be dissipated by some fresh stimulation or intoxication. Such a life, Judge William argues, is despair, and 'A' seems to agree with him. No doubt some of his despair can be described as a Byronic pose—the Judge complains that 'A' intoxicates himself with despair—but it is not only that. In the 'Diapsalmata', particularly, 'A' gives repeated expression to a pervasive sense of emptiness in his life, and a lack of reason for going on living.

---

[22] A. MacIntyre, *After Virtue: A Study in Moral Theory* (London, 1981), 41.

My life is absolutely meaningless. When I consider the different periods into which it falls, it seems like the word 'Schnur' in the dictionary, which means in the first place, a string, in the second, a daughter-in-law. The only thing lacking is that the word 'schnur' should mean in the third place a camel, in the fourth, a dust brush.[23]

'A' is thus aware of his tendency to psychological disintegration, of which the Judge warns him, 'it might end with your nature being resolved into a multiplicity, that you really might become many, become, like those unhappy demoniacs, a legion, and you thus would have lost the inmost and holiest thing of all in a man, the unifying power of personality.'[24]

Judge William is prepared to describe even the attitude of immediate aestheticism as one of 'despair', even if it is unconscious despair. By this, he means that the aesthete's happiness rests on something accidental, external to him, over which he has no control. If he is deprived of this condition of happiness, then he despairs—or, Kierkegaard would say—the despair that was latent in him becomes manifest. But the Judge's main concern is with 'A' 's reflective aestheticism. Floating in a sea of possibilities, but without committing himself to the realization of any of them, 'A' is conscious of despair; yet he can still evade it by turning his very despair into an interesting pose, a possibility to be explored. Judge William, accordingly, demands that he stop toying with despair, and despairs in earnest. Only by confronting the nullity and emptiness of a life lived without direction and purpose, can one gain the strength of will necessary for choosing to become a self, to submit oneself to the discipline of working for long-term projects irrespective of one's immediate inclinations.

But can the aesthete not give his life coherence and direction by choosing to 'will one thing'? In a way, Judge William is prepared to admit, he can. The aesthete is aware of the multiplicity of conflicting urges in his soul. 'His soul is like a plot of ground in which all sorts of herbs are planted, all with the same claim to thrive; his self consists of this multifariousness, and he has no self which is higher than this. If . . . he has the aesthetic seriousness . . . he will see that all cannot possibly thrive equally, so he will choose.'[25]

[23] *E/O* i. 35.   [24] *E/O* ii. 164.   [25] Ibid. 229–30.

Even this aesthetic seriousness, which, without concerning itself ethically, discovers one particular ability or talent or even relationship, and throws itself wholeheartedly into cultivating that, at the expense of other possibilities—even this, the Judge says, may be 'profitable to a man'.[26] But there remains something whimsical, accidental, about such aesthetic choice. It discovers one ability and cultivates that, but it has no criteria as to what it should cultivate and what it should neglect. The 'serious' aesthete chooses consistently to follow his strongest disposition, rather than whatever impulse is strongest at the time, but he is still not in control of himself. His possession of a particular talent is an accidental matter. Though he thinks that 'Satisfaction in life, and enjoyment is sought in the development of this talent', he cannot enjoy the self-possession of the ethicist, for 'the condition for satisfaction in life is the talent itself, a condition which is not posited by the individual.'[27]

As for the reflective aesthete like 'A', he has made no decisive choice, yet he is committed to a way of life as surely as anyone else. He is living a certain kind of life; he is influenced by some kinds of consideration and not by others; he experiences a wide variety of possibilities—but not those of ethical life: he does not know the satisfaction of working patiently at some task until it is accomplished, overcoming one's momentary disinclinations along the way. He has drifted into the aesthetic life, and continues to drift in it; but, for all his self-assured individualism, he is not in control of himself. He has never chosen to live in this way—how can one make a decisive choice to exclude decisive choice from one's life?—but is nevertheless deeply enmeshed in this lifestyle. 'Aesthetic seriousness' may be profitable to 'A' as a first step; but he can only come to freedom and self-possession by choosing the ethical.

This, as I see it, is the argument of *Either/Or*. It is clearly more reminiscent of Plato's and Aristotle's ethical writings than it is of Hume's or Kant's, and it is interestingly close to the Hegelian idea of social morality. I want now to discuss the issues raised by this argument, without continuing detailed references to Kierkegaard's texts, but attempting to relate his ideas to certain debates in contemporary philosophy.

[26] *E/O* ii. 230.   [27] Ibid. 187.

3.2. RECONSTRUCTING THE ETHICAL ARGUMENT

In this section I shall attempt to provide a critical reconstruction
of the argument just outlined, discussing in the process the
work of several contemporary philosophers. I begin (3.2.1) by
elucidating the underlying concept of selfhood or personal
identity with which Kierkegaard is concerned. I shall then
(3.2.2) explore the central argument that selfhood can be
achieved only through commitment to projects, saying something
about the social setting of these projects (3.2.3), before raising
the issue of the kind of projects to which the ethical individual
should commit himself. In 3.2.4 I shall discuss a strategy for
bypassing this problem by developing an ethics that is centrally
concerned with the virtues necessary for success in any project,
and attempt to assess the limitations of this strategy. Finally
(3.2.5), I shall mention briefly a possible objection to what I have
said so far.

3.2.1. *Selfhood and Personal Identity*

A self in Kierkegaard's sense is not something that one is
automatically, from birth. Rather, one is born with a capacity, a
potentiality, for being a self, and it is up to each individual to
choose to actualize this potential, or to dissipate and lose it. The
ethical individual, Judge William writes, 'has himself as a task,
in such a sort that the task is principally to order, cultivate,
temper, enkindle, repress, in short to bring about a proportionality in the soul, a harmony, which is the fruit of the
personal virtues'.[28] Each of us starts with a certain complex of
talents, dispositions, inclinations, which can be traced back to
our genetic inheritance, our individual upbringing, the culture
in which we grew up; the ethical task is to organize this raw
material into a coherent personality.

If we approach it with these concerns in mind, the problem of
personal identity can be seen in an interestingly new light. The
problem that has exercised English-speaking philosophers at
any rate, from Locke and Butler to Nozick and Parfit, is that of
determining the essence of a person. In virtue of what, do we

[28] Ibid. 267.

say that a person at one time is the same person that he was at a previous time? How is personal identity retained through change? Is it? There is usually, of course, no great practical problem in identifying someone as the same person at different times; the trouble is that ingenious thought-experiments have been constructed to show that circumstances could arise in which our ordinary criteria of personal identity—bodily similarity, physical continuity, persistence of memories, dispositions, etc.—all seem to break down. They fail to give clear answers, or, if they do, these answers seem to be incompatible with deep-seated intuitions.

Considerations such as these have led Derek Parfit to deny that there is any 'deep fact' about personal identity. There are just the greater and lesser continuities of memory, disposition, etc. He does not, of course, deny that we are sometimes justified in speaking of personal identity, but he argues that it is a far more relative matter than we are inclined to believe; it may be much more a matter of convention than we realize whether or not we say that some person at 'T' is the same as a person at 'T1'. Parfit seems keen to confront us with a sharp either/or: either we accept a quasi-Cartesian view (such as Swinburne's), or we become reductionists about personal identity, holding that all talk about persons can be translated without exception into talk about bodies and brains and mental states. 'Though persons exist, we could give a *complete* description of reality *without* claiming that persons exist.'[29] But this hardly follows from just rejecting the idea of the Cartesian Ego. It is in between Cartesianism and Parfit's radical reductionism that the most plausible and natural ways of thinking about personal identity are to be found. For one thing, Parfit and the Cartesians seem to agree in overlooking the continuity that exists in our lives simply by virtue of each of us being a distinct animal organism, which grows, matures, and decays as organisms do. I am not a Cartesian Ego, and strange, science-fiction type events could happen to me which would break down my existing personal identity. But, in their absence, I remain a psycho-physical individual, enjoying continuity in space through time, possessing certain memories, dispositions, etc. Kierkegaard is not interested

[29] D. Parfit, *Reasons and Persons* (Oxford, 1985), 212.

in ontological questions about a Cartesian Ego, or in science-fiction counterfactuals; he is concerned with the flesh and blood individual as he exists now. And the question that Kierkegaard asks is how this individual can become a self in his sense; an integrated personality. Parfitian considerations can be useful in making this question vivid to us (though I am far from wanting to endorse all of Parfit's arguments), in that they help to undermine the idea of the self as something simply given, and stress instead the chains of psychological continuity as the basis for talk of personal identity. And, as Parfit says, these links may be more or less strong, there may be more or less continuity in an individual's life. Therefore, personal identity is a matter of degree. Parfit himself concludes that the degree is a pretty low one, and strangely underestimates the amount of continuity in people's lives.[30]

Despite Parfit's exaggerations, one can recognize that there is some point to his talk about 'successive selves'.

The distinction between successive selves can be made by reference to . . . the degree of psychological connectedness. Since this connectedness is a matter of degree, the drawing of these distinctions can be left to the choice of the speaker . . . when the connections have been markedly reduced—when there has been a significant change of character, or style of life, or of beliefs and ideals—we might say 'It was not I who did that, but an earlier self.'[31]

Such talk is not just a philosophical innovation—we do say, for instance, that someone has become 'a changed man'. Scott Fitzgerald writes, with reference to certain moments of crisis in a person's life: 'A man does not recover from such jolts—he becomes a different person and, eventually, the new person finds new things to care about.'[32] Parfit quotes passages from

---

[30] He thinks that, if he were being faced with torture in the near future, he would be able to cheer up—a bit—by thinking of his 'combined spectrum' thought-experiment (ibid. §86), in which it becomes 'an empty question whether I am about to die' (ibid. 282). This looks like a confusion: things may happen which baffle our intuitions as to whom they are happening, but, if I am sitting in a cell awaiting torture the next morning, this case is quite unproblematic; there is no doubt at all about who is going to be tortured—I am.

[31] Ibid. 304–5. Note that I cautiously restrict myself to saying that there is 'some point' to this way of speaking. For further discussion of 'short-term selves', see below, pp. 91 ff.

[32] F. Scott Fitzgerald, 'The Crack-Up', in *The Crack-Up, with Other Pieces and Stories* (Harmondsworth, 1983), 47.

Proust and Solzhenitsyn[33] with a similar import. What this way of talking tends to overlook, however, is the fact that the person one is now is the result of one's past history, of one's 'previous selves', and cannot be understood without reference to them. I will say more about this below.

The degree of psychological continuity in a person's life may be greater or less; for Kierkegaard, this means that a stable, coherent personality, a personal identity that does persist through time and change and 'jolts', is something that must be achieved, struggled for. And it is by committing oneself to projects that one's selfhood is developed.

3.2.2. *Projects and the Unity of Life*

What do I mean by 'projects'? I shall approach a consideration of the concept of a project by starting with some remarks about purposive action in general. I have no intention of developing a full-blown theory of action here, but I do want to stress the point that, to describe an action, is to tell a story. Using what is admittedly a rather simplistic or idealized model, one starts with a decision to act in order to bring about some desired state of affairs, passes on to the action itself, and concludes with the attainment of the goal. The 'action itself' becomes intelligible by being set in the context of its desired result, and of the decision to act so as to bring that result about. The intelligibility of the present action depends on its looking back to the past and ahead to the future. Of course, as I said, this model is simplistic. To be intentional, an action need not be preceded by any Cartesian *introspectibilium*. Indeed, it is only by seeing what (in)action follows from it that we can distinguish between a genuine intention and an idle wish. Nor, of course, is the goal of the action always something distinct from the action itself. (For example: the goal is to savour the taste of some food; this is not distinct from the activity of eating it, which is the means to that end.) But these are familiar points in post-Wittgensteinian philosophy of action.

So, in purposive action I am looking back to the past and ahead to the future, and it is this wider temporal context that gives my action its intelligibility—both to me and to others—by

[33] Parfit, *Reasons and Persons*, 305.

showing it to be a response to a situation as it has developed, and intended to alter that situation in a way that it is reasonable for me to desire. A single action gains intelligibility as it is put in the context of a whole series of actions. Indeed, we might regard a single action as an abstraction from a whole pattern of action; a report of a single action is an episode in a longer story. If we take 'He did y because he wanted x' as explaining why someone acted as he did, we still have to ask why he wanted x, why he thought that y would help him get what he wanted; and then there are the further questions that are raised by those answers. As we trace this process back, we situate this action within a whole context of aims, desires, dispositions, projects, ambitions, and aversions on the part of the agent, together with the story of his life, his social background, and relationships. This process can continue indefinitely; as historians know, a cut-off point has to be found at which it is said that further material is no longer relevant to understanding the particular action on which they focus—but any such point has to be chosen more or less arbitrarily.

What I have been saying is related to Anscombe's point that an action can be characterized under a variety of descriptions; as we build in more context, our understanding of what the original action is changes. To use her example, we understand more and more of what is going on as we move from 'he is moving his arm up and down', to 'he is working the pump', to 'he is supplying the house with water', to 'he is poisoning the inhabitants', to 'he is assassinating the Party leaders'.[34] If no further context could be built in, if we could find no other description than 'he is moving his arm up and down', then we would not be able to understand his action. Even to say that he is mad is to create a context that can be further elaborated.[35] As MacIntyre says, the category of 'intelligible action' is more basic than that of 'action'—an unintelligible action is a bodily movement that fails as a candidate for the status of intelligible action because it cannot be made part of a narrative, cannot be fitted into a context.

Now, 'projects' in my sense are what provide the context

[34] G. E. M. Anscombe, *Intention*, 2nd edn. (Oxford, 1979), §23.
[35] Cf. Anscombe's remarks on the intelligibility of a demand for a saucer of mud (ibid. §37).

within which a person's actions can make sense—to himself and
to others. A project is a pattern of purposive action, extending
over some period of time—perhaps indefinitely—which aims at
the achievement of certain psychologically understandable
goals. Projects are generally embedded in larger-scale projects
like Russian dolls—I am going to the bank now, so that I will be
able to get food for tonight's meal. But that project is embedded
in my larger-scale project of simply staying alive, and in
reasonable comfort. That is a project which absorbs all of us for a
large part of the time, nearly all the time in many people's lives.
But what I am concerned with here are the projects on which an
individual embarks when he has satisfied his basic needs; not
the ones by which he simply stays alive, but those which make
his life worth living. Examples of such projects would be
marriage, friendship, the raising of children, artistic creativity,
scientific work, a career, involvement in some hobby or sport (if
this is taken as seriously as some people do take it). What I am
getting at is closely related to what Bernard Williams says about
the 'ground projects', which give meaning to a person's life and
continuity to his character. He speaks of 'the idea of a man's
ground projects providing the motive force which propels him
into the future and gives him a reason for living';[36] and also of
'the idea of one person's having a character in the sense of
having projects and categorical desires with which that person is
identified'.[37] It is by drawing on this—distinctly Kierkegaardian—
notion of character that Williams criticizes Parfit's attempt to
dissolve us into successive short-term selves.[38]

Nietzsche once remarked[39] that he who possesses the 'why?'
of his life can put up with almost any 'how'. What matters is not
searching for 'happiness' ('Only the Englishman does that'), but
to have the sense that one's life has some purpose in it, that
one's actions are significant. Kierkegaard's thesis, as I understand
it, is that this significance is conferred by the projects to which
an individual commits himself. In so far as he is acting to further
the projects to which he is committed, he has continuity in his

[36] B. Williams, 'Persons, Characters and Morality', in his *Moral Luck*
(Cambridge, 1981), 13.   [37] Ibid. 14.   [38] Ibid. 5–10.
[39] F. Nietzsche, *Twilight of the Idols*, trans. R. J. Hollingdale, publ. with *The
Antichrist* (Harmondsworth, 1982), 23. ('Maxims and Arrows', no. 12; see also
no. 44: 'Formula of my happiness: a yes, a no, a straight line, a goal').

life: in his action he looks back to the past development of his project—perhaps, though not necessarily, to an initial moment of decision for it—and he looks forward to its continued development into the future. He acts now, when the action is a contribution to a certain project, in response to the project's progression to date—this gives him the situation to which he responds—and the present action carries the project forward, aims towards its continued development through further problems and sub-projects. So long as a person is acting in furtherance of projects that have significance for him, then he can be said to feel that his life has purpose. And Nietzsche is psychologically right here—it is this that matters (even to the English) more than 'happiness', which, taken by itself in its naked generality, is a rather empty concept.

According to Pascal, most of the troubles and sufferings of the world can be traced to the inability of people simply to stay contentedly in their rooms.[40] But if we imagine someone who does just stay in his room—has no job, no friendships, no intellectual or artistic interests, no hobbies, participates in no sports, no political or religious organizations—this seems to be the paradigm of a meaningless existence (even if it is not necessarily an unhappy one; the person in question may watch television or take drugs all day, and be content). Why, after all, is unemployment felt to be such a curse even apart from the financial deprivation that it involves, and even if the work that is missed was, or would be, tedious? What is ennui (as opposed to mere passing states of boredom) but the feeling that there is no point in any action, that one has no purpose? And, as Schopenhauer points out,[41] people will throw themselves into any sort of activity, however pointless or even unpleasant it may seem, in order to escape the threat of ennui. He also saw that, although we often propose a specific goal that we aim to reach, we are not infrequently rather indifferent to the goal itself;[42]

---

[40] B. Pascal, *Pensées*, trans. A. J. Krailsheimer (Harmondsworth, 1986), §136.
[41] A. Schopenhauer, *The World as Will and Representation*, trans. E. F. J. Payne, 2 vols. (New York, 1969), i. §57.
[42] 'The goal was only apparent: possession takes away its charm. The wish, the need, appears again on the scene under a new form; if it does not, then dreariness, emptiness and boredom follow . . .' (ibid. 314). Of course, this is also one of Pascal's favourite themes (cf. Pascal, *Pensées*, §132–9, in particular). For both Pascal and Schopenhauer, these observations serve as proof that there is

what matters is that we have something to aim for—no matter
what—so that we may feel we are acting purposively. We are
teleological creatures, but our *tele* are often—I do not say
always!—unimportant to us in themselves. And if—as so
often—we fail to realize this, then the sense of disillusion and
emptiness that Schopenhauer describes so vividly is apt to
supervene when we reach our goals. This is at least one reason
why a goal does not need to be described fully or vividly in
order to have a great influence on us and to become the object of
our striving. Note the paucity and vagueness of descriptions of
heaven in religious literature—especially as compared to those
of hell!

People have, then, a need to feel that they are acting for
purposes. (These do not need to be conceived on any simple
model of means and ends—the examples that I have given of
projects are characteristically of patterns of activity that have no
'point' outside themselves. A friendship that has a purpose
beyond itself is not a friendship at all, but some other
relationship.) One can ask of anyone who has just performed
some action, why he did that. And the answer will typically
situate the action in a context of aims, desires, ambitions,
relationships, and duties; descriptions of the past events to
which it was a response or of which it was the outcome, and of
the future events which it is hoped it will bring—or help to
bring—about. It is when no such context can be provided that
we find the action inexplicable—and therefore puzzling, un-
canny, frightening. The power and value of psychoanalytic
therapy lies in its capacity to tell stories about patients that make
their actions seem meaningful, that give intelligibility back to
them. A psychoanalyst is confronted by the apparent nonsense
of a dream or of a hysteric's obsessional behaviour; he proceeds
to interpret these phenomena, to show that they do make sense.
And this means turning the description of the dream or of the
strange actions from a mere enumeration of events, unconnected
by any apparent logic, into a real narrative. One event follows

something profoundly absurd about the existence of most people, if they spend
so much time pursuing what they do not particularly want to have. But this is
not a necessary conclusion; why should we not find our happiness in striving
rather than in possession? The outlook summarized in Blake's aphorism 'Energy
is Eternal Delight' is, of course, the antithesis of Schopenhauer's.

from another in these reconstructed narratives, and they are all recognizably the outcome of the patient's desires and aims; that is, his unconscious desires and aims. And these in turn are made intelligible by an account of their genesis, perhaps in early childhood.

Of course, there are various different schools of psychoanalytic therapy, each of which will read the evidence of a patient's actions and dreams differently. Perhaps, though, we should not worry too much about which account is the true one (the one that corresponds to the psychological facts)—it is, rather, a matter of interpretation, and might be compared with literary criticism rather than with an idealized physics. (I say 'idealized', as I suspect that physics is itself much more of a hermeneutical discipline than is generally acknowledged in our philosophical tradition.) There are many literary critics, and they do not all agree about the texts that they read. There is no such thing as the finally correct interpretation of *Hamlet* or *The Possessed*, or *The Castle*. But this does not mean that anything goes. There are good, insightful interpretations, and crass, ludicrous ones; similarly with psychoanalysis.[43] And here one suspects that what matters to the patient, what effects the cure, is that his behaviour has been given *a* meaning—never mind about *the*

---

[43] 'The [Freudian] investigatory procedure has, in effect, a strong affinity with the disciplines of textual interpetation.' (P. Ricœur, 'The Question of Proof in Freud's Psychoanalytic Writings', in his *Hermeneutics and the Human Sciences*, ed. and trans. J. B. Thomson (Cambridge, 1984), 255.) It is Ricœur who has most thoroughly developed this hermeneutical account of psychoanalysis (cf. esp. his *Freud and Philosophy*, trans. D. Savage (New Haven, Conn., and London, 1970). It should be said, though, that he does not regard psychoanalysis purely as a hermeneutical discipline; the 'texts' with which it deals are ones that have been distorted by the operation of certain 'mechanisms', which call for a more 'objective', theoretical understanding: 'The interpretative decoding of symptoms and dreams goes beyond a simply philological hermeneutics, insofar as it is the very meaning of the mechanisms distorting the texts that requires explanation.' (Ricœur, 'The Question of Proof', 260.)

I should say that my attitude to the various schools of psychology is not wholly relativistic. The Kierkegaardian ideas that I am developing in this chapter are themselves much closer to Adler's 'individual psychology', with its stress on people's need for meaningful projects, than they are to orthodox Freudian psychoanalysis. From a Kierkegaardian perspective, one can see Freud—with his fundamentally hedonistic and asocial understanding of human nature—as the psychologist of the aesthetic life, and Adler as the psychologist of the ethical. For the sake of symmetry, one might include Jung as the psychologist of the religious—although Jung's and Kierkegaard's ideas about religion are rather different.

(correct) meaning. What he could not explain to himself before has now become intelligible; he can tell a story about his life that restores to it a coherent sense. Previously fragmented events can now be understood as fitting into the pattern of a narrative.

The situation is not, I think, so different with normal (non-neurotic) people; we just need less specialist help in constructing our narratives. I understand my current situation in terms of my past decisions and actions, inactions and indecisions, as a result of which I am where I am now; and in terms of my plans, projects, and commitments for the future on which I am working now. And, again, all this material can be interpreted in various ways; different stories can be told about my life from various viewpoints—religious, psychoanalytic, sociological, or whatever. A biography—even if it is an autobiography—can never be written once and for all, any more than any other kind of history can be. There is always room for different emphases, new ways of interpreting and making sense of the data, of seeing past events as fitting into new patterns. Again, as the analogy with literary criticism makes clear, this does not mean that we should fall into some hopeless relativism which would ascribe as much and as little weight to any story that was told about our lives.[44] But it is important to remember here that we do not just make up stories about our lives as we look back on them—we live them in narrative terms. I see my current planning and acting and deliberating as following from past events and as liable to lead to definite future ones; not simply as a matter of blind causality, but through the realization or frustration of intentions that have their intelligible basis in my desires, wishes, ideals. Suppose for instance, that I have been converted to some political ideal, have joined a group or party, and am aiming to bring about certain changes. This is a narrative that I act out as I live; my present actions are intended to help realize future changes, and my motivation to work for them derives from, perhaps, some shocking experience in the past which altered my previous attitudes. I see myself now as acting from a clear-headed perception of the nature of society. Maybe

[44] 'As the logic of text interpretation suggests, there is a specific plurivocity belonging to the meaning of human action. Human action, too, is a limited field of possible constructions.' (P. Ricœur, 'The Model of the Text: Meaningful Action Considered as a Text', in his *Hermeneutics and the Human Sciences*, 213.)

when I look back on all this in the future, I will see it as the folly of a romantic; that is, I will tell a very different story about this period of my life. But I will still have to identify with my younger self, for what I will be then will be the outcome of a process that has carried me from what I am now, and this will include the various experiences that influenced me to turn away from my current course of political activism. And I—or anyone else—may reflect on whether this story is one of maturing or of moral corruption.

This example is (intentionally) similar to Parfit's example of the Russian nobleman,[45] but it is meant to suggest what is wrong with his talk of short-term selves who can regard one another as alien beings. The middle-aged nobleman cannot quite so regard his younger self—at least not without an element of self-deception and hyprocrisy; however absurd those ideals may seem to him now, what he is now is the result of a development from what he was then. Hence Fitzgerald, for all his talk of the 'jolts' that turned him (more than once) into a different person, looks back on his past life in order to understand his present predicament. St Augustine, after his conversion, did not dismiss his previous experiences as worthless, alien, but was concerned to trace his progress towards conversion, to understand his past life from the perspective that he had obtained at the time of writing the *Confessions*. Nor can the young nobleman quite disregard his later self. I may perhaps have reason to believe that a process of torture or brainwashing would cause me to adopt ideals and beliefs utterly repugnant to me now—Nazism or something similar, for example—and I might choose to kill myself rather than let that happen to me. But if I believe that my views will change without drastic external pressure being applied, how can I regard this? If I really believe this to be a process of appalling moral corruption that inevitably affects everyone with age, then suicide might be the only answer, as it might be to the onset of an incurable and painful disease. But if I just regard it as probable that my views

---

[45] Parfit, *Reasons and Persons*, §110. This 19th-cent. Russian is supposed to have socialist ideals, and has therefore decided to give the land that he will inherit in the future to the peasants. Because he suspects that his ideals may fade as time goes by, he arranges things so that he will be unable to revoke this decision, should he—or his future self—want to do so in the future.

will develop and mellow with age, then that implies a certain relativism, which will affect the passion with which I hold them now. If I regard my views not as the truth about society that I am determined to hold on to at all costs, but just as the typical opinions of a naïve youth, then I simply cannot take them so seriously even now. But if I think of them as being the truth—which is necessary if I am to hold to them now with passion—then it is hard to see how I can fatalistically believe that I will abandon them as I grow older. Even if I recognize that there will be increasing temptations to apostatize as time passes, this should merely harden my determination to remain loyal to the truth, not to await with resignation the death of my old personality with its ideals, while developing mechanisms to thwart the designs of my cynical successor-self.

Personal identity is not a matter of the persistence of an unchanging Cartesian substance; it depends on the degree of continuity in an individual's life. Clearly, this may vary to a greater or lesser extent, but, even when the continuity is interrupted by a major jolt, it is misleading to suggest that we should think in terms of separate selves. The dramatic events—or gradual accumulation of undramatic events—which transform someone's personality, ideals, outlook, must themselves be understood in a context, and that is provided by the past life of the person in question. A story of remarkable and unexpected upheavals may be a coherent narrative, as much as an account of uninterrupted continuity may be. Nevertheless, the narrative structure of an individual's life—and thus its unity—may break down. One may be unable to make any intelligible narrative out of the events of a life. One can, of course, enumerate the events in chronological order; but there may be little 'logic' in the sequence thus set down. This is what happens in Kafka's novels—his heroes are dragged through a series of events which they cannot fit into any intelligible order or pattern (though there does at least appear to be an order that is known to the Court or the Castle, but which 'K' is never able to make sense of). On a (usually) lighter note, the same is true of picaresque novels. These can be read almost as collections of short stories, each episode a coherent narrative in itself, but only minimally connected with the others. But if we are dealing with a genuine novel, as opposed to a collection of weakly linked stories, then the various episodes will contribute to a wider story, which is that of the development of the character(s) whose adventures they all are.

Narrative structure can also break down in real life; this is what—according to Kierkegaard—happens in the life of the aesthete. As I have insisted above, human beings are teleological: we need purposes. And simply staying alive requires purposive action that fills most of the lives of most people. Where there is purposive action, there is narrative; and the aesthete is far from inactive, as we have seen. On the contrary, he throws himself into all kinds of activities, perhaps with great frenzy and enthusiasm. But there is always the proviso that, should his whim change, the aesthete may 'sheer off at will'[46] from whatever it is that he is involved in. Accordingly, the story of his life can only be some kind of picaresque. There will be a series of different narratives of different episodes, but they will not add up to a single narrative; they will just remain a series of episodes. This is the sense in which the aesthete lacks any stable personal identity; his life is without continuity.

3.2.3. Personal Projects and Social Life

For one's life to acquire this continuity, for one to develop a personal identity, it is necessary to commit oneself to projects. To embark on a significant project, from which one does not 'sheer off' when the whim takes one, is to give one's life at least some aspect of secure narrative structure. The story of one's life is (in part) the story of the development of whatever project one has adopted (there will normally, of course, be several). But this means accepting that the project confers an identity on oneself, which means rejecting, or at least qualifying, the disengaged idea of the pure autonomous self, distinct from all social roles, relationships, and commitments. If someone's marriage is a significant project, it will involve that person thinking of him- or herself *as* a husband or wife; if someone's job is significant for him, it will involve him thinking of himself *as* a doctor, engineer, or whatever; if someone's political or religious commitments are significant, he must see himself *as* a Christian, a socialist, or whatever. The contrast is with someone who sees

[46] *E/O* i. 292.

himself as an individual who is, perhaps, married, who has a job, who votes for a party or attends a Church, but who sees all these things as ultimately external, contingent relations into which he enters without them thereby constituting him as the person that he is. I mentioned before Bernard Williams's example of the bank clerk who cannot deny that he is a bank clerk, but who can nevertheless be said not to think of himself *as* a bank clerk. It seems that most—if not all—projects that are significant enough to give one's life a purpose and meaning will involve at least some degree of social interaction, and will therefore have some kind of social definition. As such, they are what MacIntyre calls 'practices': 'By a "practice", I am going to mean any coherent and complex form of socially established cooperative human activity through which goods internal to that form of activity are realised in the course of trying to achieve those standards of excellence which are appropriate to, and partially definitive of, that form of activity.'[47] As examples of such practices, he gives 'arts, sciences, games, politics in the Aristotelian sense, the making and sustaining of family life'.[48] One might imagine a hermit whose project is to live a life of isolated self-sufficiency out in the wild, but—allowing for the possibility of occasional exceptions to this rule—one can say that, in choosing to commit oneself to a project, one is accepting a certain social role. A project such as marriage, being a scientist, or a bank clerk, or a Catholic, involves participation in an institution or a set of institutions. What it is to be any of those things is quite clearly defined in social practice. Philippa Foot and others have argued against ethical non-cognitivism by pointing out that not just any behaviour can be called, for example, 'rude' or 'kind';[49] similarly, not just anything counts as being a wife, a scientist, or a socialist. Certainly, definitions of such roles are not immutable, but, in changing an institution, one must start from where it is. An artist may extend the limits of what is considered to be art by some bold innovation, and thus extend the limits of what is considered to be artistic activity; but not just any activity can be regarded as 'artistic' without the

---

[47] MacIntyre, *After Virtue*, 175.   [48] Ibid.
[49] Cf. P. Foot, 'Moral Arguments', in her *Virtues and Vices, and Other Essays in Moral Philosophy* (Oxford, 1978), and 'Moral Beliefs', in *Virtues and Vices*.

concept becoming empty. (Arguably, this has now happened.) The concept of marriage can be, and has been, extended. Does a marriage require a religious ceremony? Or just a civil ceremony? Or any initial ceremony at all? (Consider the development of the concept of a 'common-law marriage', which now has some legal as well as social force.) But, clearly, not every relationship between a man and a woman can be counted as marriage. Of course, within a marriage, the conception of the roles of husband and wife has changed a good deal. But though the definitions of social roles are flexible, they do exist—even in the case of those which do not have a particular institutional status, such as friendship. In choosing to embark on a project, I am accepting that a description of the relevant role applies to me, that I can be correctly described as a wife, a lawyer, a Muslim, or whatever it may be. I may not accept all the characterizations of what a good x is, but, if my wish to be considered an x at all is sincere, I cannot reject them all. A description of a role carries with it the standards of assessment of a person trying to play that role—and, if he truly wishes to be considered thus, then he cannot ignore those standards and invent his own way of being a husband, a doctor, a socialist, a historian, without reference to the way in which those roles are defined in his society. Similarly, he cannot simply adopt any project, regardless of whether or not there is any institutional space for it in his society. I cannot just choose to become a witch-doctor, even if I wear a grass skirt, perform ritualistic dances, and examine chicken entrails. I still would not *be* a witch doctor until some group accepted me *as* their witch-doctor, and came to me for advice and treatment, while eschewing more conventional forms of religion and medicine. In other words, we would have to form a community in which there was an institutional role of witch-doctor, before I could legitimately regard myself as being one.

So far I have mentioned projects that one chooses, and I have made a close connection between these and institutional social roles. But not all such roles can be said to have been chosen. For a start, the relationship that most people have with their parents is of great formulative importance, but it cannot be said to have been chosen. Furthermore, I am born not just into a family, but into a nation and a culture. The simple fact that I grow up

speaking one particular language initiates me into a certain
tradition, a way of seeing and evaluating the world. Of course, I
can rebel against the national and cultural values with which I
was brought up, as I can rebel against my parents, but I cannot
simply shake them off. That I am English, that I am European,
an inheritor of a certain culture: these things are part of my
identity—I cannot just shrug them off as if they were alien to
me. Again, though there is an element of truth in Bradley's
heady rhetoric about the individual being constituted by his
society, we do not have to draw nationalistic or totalitarian
conclusions from this; that I am of necessity immersed in my
own culture does not render me incapable of criticizing it or of
appreciating other cultures. Indeed, the study of another culture
may become a project which absorbs much of my life and
becomes of the greatest significance for me. And, of course, one
should not think of any sophisticated culture as a monolithic
block: there are various different—conflicting and complement-
ary—cross-currents in our culture, which can be played off
against one another, extended, or enriched with material from
other cultures.

Nevertheless, it remains true that, as a child grows to self-
consciousness, it finds itself with an identity that is ready-made,
based on membership of groups—family, cultural, religious,
regional, national, sexual—which it has not chosen. On Kierkegaard's analysis, the crowd man passively accepts the identity
given him in this way and the standards of behaviour that go
with membership of the various groups. He will then enter into
other relationships—work, marriage—which he can be said to
choose for himself, but which may in fact be largely determined
by external factors. The aesthete is one who becomes sufficiently
self-conscious about his socially given identity to stand back
from it. Not that he can entirely repudiate it, but he can
maintain a degree of ironic distance. The ethicist is one who
consciously re-engages in the commitments and relationships of
social life, who is willing to accept the conditions that have—
beyond his control—made him what he is. The man who
chooses himself discovers that

the self he chooses contains an endless multiplicity insomuch as it has a
history . . . in this history he stands in relation to other individuals of

the race, and to the race as a whole . . . Therefore it requires courage for a man to choose himself: for at the very time when it seems that he isolates himself most thoroughly, he is more thoroughly absorbed in the root by which he is connected with the whole . . . He repents himself back into himself, back into the family, back into the race . . .[50]

So we can choose to accept what, in any case, we cannot wholly evade—our participation in the society and the culture in which we were born and brought up; and here again we find that there are standards for being a good citizen, a good son or daughter, a good Basque, or whatever. In so far as we accept our membership of such groups, that our participation in such relationships contributes to our identities, we must accept the standards of assessment that go with them as relevant to us— which, once again, is not to say that we cannot work for their alteration, or that we must accept them blindly. Nor, indeed, is it to say that the duties derived from one set of relationships may not clash with others; there may be conflict between those deriving from different national, religious, regional, and familial commitments. But, as MacIntyre says, 'we all approach our own circumstances as bearers of a particular social identity . . . Hence, what is good for me has to be the good for one who inhabits these rôles. As such, I inherit from the past of my family, my city, my tribe, my nation, a variety of debts, inheritances, rightful expectations and allegations.'[51] This means, to give a couple of his examples, that contemporary Britons must accept a share of responsibility for the current problems in Ireland which derive from centuries of British ill government, and that white Americans must bear a share of responsibility for the conditions of blacks today.

At first sight, this looks like the logic of the terrorist, who believes that he is morally justified in murdering any national of a country whose government's policy he dislikes. But I think there is a point in what MacIntyre is saying here. If, as a contemporary Briton or American, I want to be proud of my country today, I must be ashamed of a great deal of what it was in the past. For, in so far as the nation can be said to have a cohesive identity in which I participate, this derives from its tradition, from its past, and the way in which it has developed.

[50] *E/O* ii. 220.   [51] MacIntyre, *After Virtue*, 205.

The history of the nation, with all its crimes, is what has constituted the country with which I identify today, and that history may have generated responsibilities which have to be shouldered by the nation—for instance, responsibilities of Britain towards Ireland, and of Germany towards the Jews. If I do not identify myself as British, but, say, as a member of the international proletariat, I may feel sympathy and solidarity with past victims of British governments, but no responsibility or guilt. But, even so, my position may be equivocal if I live in Britain, enjoy the benefits of so doing, speak English even; I am participating in a certain national culture which is in part founded on the atrocities for which I disclaim any share of responsibility. Similarly, I may deplore the international economic order that allocates so much of the world's resources to so few, but I remain one of those who benefit from this set-up. And not only in a direct, material sense, but in that my upbringing and education have given me a certain outlook and identity which I can never wholly repudiate, but which has come about through my participation in a culture whose economic basis I object to. But, if I do, I cannot feel devoid of all responsibility for this state of affairs myself.

The ethical individual, trying to build up a coherent, stable personality, accepts his social background in this sense. And he consciously chooses to take on projects—as a matter of long-term commitment rather than short-term whim. In this way his life acquires a continuity; his actions now have the significance of contributing to the project that he adopted in the past, and of developing it in the future. The story of his life becomes a narrative stretching across time rather than a series of episodes. Instead of giving heed now to one inclination, now to another, he orders and disciplines his desires so as to accomplish something definite in one area, to develop one set of talents fully and richly, even if it means neglecting others. For the alternative is never fully to actualize any of one's potentials.

These ideas about the ethical life drawn from the writings of Judge William, are, as I hope I have suggested, defensible and relevant to contemporary issues. But they raise a good many problems. In particular, is all of this relevant to morality as we usually understand it?

3.2.4. Projects and Virtues

So far I have followed Kierkegaard's Judge William in arguing for the need for commitment to long-term projects. But the question now arises: 'What projects?' One answer to this question which seems to have an authentically Kierkegaardian, existentialist ring to it would be to say that the important thing is to make some definite commitments, no matter to what, in order to avoid the disintegration of one's personality. This appears to lead us back into subjectivism, irrationalism, arbitrary choice; we seem to be left without the resources for judging someone's ground projects themselves as either good or evil. Before confronting this problem, I want to examine a possible way of bypassing it. This is the attempt to show that a substantive ethic can be derived from the necessity to make commitments to projects, without the projects themselves having to be specified. This is to be done by attempting to establish that the virtues, as systematically discussed by classical and medieval moral philosophy, are necessary for the conduct of any worthwhile human life, 'as health and sanity are needed'.[52] This is an Aristotelianism, without the Aristotelian conception of a single specifiable *telos* of human nature as such.

Kierkegaard, like the Aristotelians, regards projects or practices as the setting for the development and exercise of the virtues. He distinguishes[53] between personal, civic, and religious virtues. The personal virtues ('courage, valour, temperance, moderation', as Judge William rather vaguely lists them[54]) are those necessary for self-development, for success in one's projects, for living a full and satisfying life as an individual. But this is not enough for genuine fulfilment, which can only be found in society, and Judge William reproaches those classical moralists who aimed at an ideal of self-sufficiency for neglecting the civic virtues.[55] These are necessary for living in society and participating in social life. Chief amongst them is justice—and the Judge approves of Aristotle's close association of friendship with justice.[56] Aristotle goes astray, however, in stopping at social life—for him, 'the idea of the state becomes the highest idea'.[57]

[52] P. T. Geach, *The Virtues* (Cambridge, 1977), 16.
[53] *E/O* ii. 245, 266.   [54] Ibid. 245.
[55] Ibid.   [56] Ibid. 327.   [57] Ibid.

(This is not quite fair, in view of what Aristotle has to say in praise of the contemplative life.) For Judge William, though, there are also the religious virtues, which arise from the individual's relation to God; though the Judge, in contrast to Kierkegaard himself, believes that the individual relates to God not simply as an individual, but as a member of the established Church, the Christian community.

This threefold distinction can be compared with the one that Geach makes. He distinguishes between the four traditional 'cardinal' virtues—prudence, justice, temperance, and courage—and the three 'theological' virtues—faith, hope, and charity. He writes that we can all agree on seeing 'the need of the four cardinal virtues to men: these virtues are needed for any large-scale worthy enterprise'.[58] Whatever our larger world-view may be, we can all accept that these virtues are necessary for the success of any serious project to which we may commit ourselves. However, as Geach goes on to say: 'The need of men for faith, hope and charity could be established only by a far more specific determination of man's end.'[59] In other words these can be counted as genuine virtues only if Christianity gives the true account of what the human *telos* is.

Now, if we can show that the cultivation of the four cardinal virtues is necessary given any serious account of human nature and destiny, then we will have constructed a basic ethical framework to which all rational people can agree, whatever their further differences. Given that, as Kierkegaard has argued, we need to make long-term commitments to projects, it follows that we need to cultivate the four cardinal virtues as well as those further virtues that are necessary not for any project, but for the particular projects that we do choose to undertake. So, we will have a basic rational morality that holds good for everyone, whatever his or her projects may be, and the threat of subjectivism seems to subside.

As far as three of the four virtues are concerned, there seems to be little problem in providing justification for their cultivation. In Geach's words: 'We need prudence or practical wisdom for any large-scale planning . . . we need temperance in order not to be deflected from our long-term and large-scale goals by

[58] Geach, *The Virtues*, 16.   [59] Ibid. 17.

seeking short-term satisfactions. And we need courage in order to persevere in face of setbacks, weariness, difficulties and dangers.'[60] And I think there is another virtue worth adding to the list. It is discussed by Kierkegaard's Judge William when criticizing 'A' 's use of his imagination to lift himself out of his concrete situation, and by Kierkegaard in his own right in *Purity of Heart* and elsewhere. Amongst modern writers, Iris Murdoch has done most to stress its importance. It is not clearly defined, and has no agreed name, but it could be described as a certain kind of honesty—not towards other people (that is a part of justice, which I will discuss later), but with oneself. It is a refusal to be blinded by one's desires and wishes to the extent of seeing things as they are not. In order to carry through any project, I need to be able to weigh up my situation realistically, to understand what other people are thinking and feeling, and to know what I really want and really feel. Instead we all too often see things as we want to see them, without pausing to look closely enough to check if that is how they really are. As a result, we may come to do disastrous harm to others or to ourselves. One might place this virtue under the general heading of prudence, but there is a difference of emphasis, at least, between prudence as usually understood and this virtue of honest perception, of refusal to lock ourselves into a cocoon of self-gratifying fantasy. Murdoch writes that 'Morality, goodness, is a form of realism . . . the chief enemy of excellence in morality (and also in art) is personal fantasy: the tissue of self-aggrandising and consoling wishes and dreams which prevents one seeing what is there outside one.'[61] My conception differs from hers, in that I do not want to make it the key to morality as a whole, and, indeed, I do not want to presuppose ideas about morality and the value of unselfishness. Even for the most selfish projects, I need to see things clearly and honestly, as they are. But I think that Murdoch has done us a service in stressing the importance of honest perception.

This brings us to the problem of justice. The virtues that are easy to justify are, of course, the self-regarding ones. But what of the other-regarding virtues? Geach writes: 'We need justice to

---

[60] Ibid. 16.
[61] I. Murdoch, *The Sovereignty of Good* (London, 1970), 59.

secure cooperation and mutual trust among men, without which our lives would be nasty, brutish and short.'[62] This is perfectly true, but it does not quite succeed in answering the question: Why should *I* be just? As Philippa Foot says, the virtues are beneficial, but 'we must ask to whom the benefit goes, whether to the man who has the virtue, or rather to those who have to do with him?'[63] This is the old question of Plato's *Republic*; if justice is the pursuit of another man's good, why is it good for me to be just? To justify justice, if it can be done at all, is harder than it is to justify the other cardinal virtues. This suggests that Kierkegaard was right to distinguish between personal, civic, and religious virtues as three distinct categories, needing rather different treatment, instead of making Geach's twofold distinction between cardinal and theological virtues, which lumps justice together with the personal virtues.

The first line in the defence of justice is the one already mentioned above: as social beings, we need to live in society, and, for a society to exist at all, there must be recognized laws and standards to which people are willing to adhere, recognized ways of settling disputes, and so on. But just because there is a system of law, it does not necessarily follow that the system is just—unless we simply define justice as the disposition to obey whatever laws are in operation in one's society. Clearly, any system of law will put restraints on people's actions so as to prevent harm to other members of the society. But the effect of laws may be—and usually has been—simply to formalize the power relations in a society, to establish the conditions under which one group exploits another. One group may find that the best way to secure its own interests is to ensure that the lives of the members of some other groups are indeed nasty, brutish, and short.

For the purpose of this discussion, I want to imagine a society that systematically discriminates between its citizens; one in which political and economic power is monopolized by one group within the society, and used to exploit and keep in subjection all other groups. Now, such a society does have laws—even if they are different ones for rich and poor, white

[62] Geach, *The Virtues*, 16.
[63] P. Foot, 'Virtues and Vices', in her *Virtues and Vices*, 3.

and black. (They do not have to be. There may be a theoretical equality before the law which just does not function in practice.) And while the ruling classes may regard the lower orders simply as serfs or helots to be treated as they please, they may recognize obligations to them. But they will not treat them as equals. Clearly, however, they will have to so treat their fellow rulers, recognizing amongst themselves mutual claims of right. If the rulers did nothing but stab one another in the back, and could not even count on one another's co-operation in suppressing peasant revolts, the society would soon crumble. So there is a good reason why members of one particular group should be just to another (though we still have the problem of the cunning hypocrite, who is unjust in the assurance that most people will remain sufficiently fair-minded to keep the society on which he is a parasite ticking over). However, there is no reason why they should be just to those outside the group.

One might suggest[64] that, once we have acquired the concepts of justice, mutual aid, honesty, and so forth, we can develop them beyond their initial limited scope, and ask why they should not be extended to govern our behaviour towards those outside our community. This is the principle of universalization: if I make different moral judgements in two cases, I must be able to point to a relevant difference in the cases. Well, if, as a child in a caste-society, I am trained to help others in my caste, tell them the truth, and so forth, I may come to ask: Why is it right for me to help 'A' and not 'B'? And I will be told: 'B' is not one of us. Historically, the chances are that I will find this a convincing argument, but I might not, and I might then start being nice to 'B'. However, if I am coldly rational about it, and think of morality as a matter of serving my own best long-term interests and those of my community, then I may realize that it is perfectly rational for me to help 'A' and not 'B'. We—the ruling élite—need to stick together so as to keep the rest in their place and live off their labour. Accordingly, Hare's rather optimistic attempt to argue a South African racist into equal moral concern for blacks and whites is unlikely to get far.[65] I think Hare would

---

[64] See e.g. P. F. Strawson, 'Social Morality and Individual Ideal', *Philosophy* (1960), 8 ff.

[65] See R. M. Hare, *Freedom and Reason* (Oxford, 1963), ch. 11.

say that, if he argues as I have represented above, the South
African would be outside morality altogether, and Hare's ethical
subjectivism means that he does not think that someone can be
argued into morality from scratch. But my point is that my
imagined oligarch has given a perfectly rational justification of a
limited morality—both the morality itself and its—rather strict—
limits.

Of course, the weakness of this rather sceptical argument so
far is that it takes the stance of a rational individual asking: What
can I get out of justice? But, as I have argued above, we are
social creatures who flourish in, become attached to, and
identify with particular societies, act justly towards our fellow
members of those societies, and forego opportunities to do well
for ourselves at the expense of the general good because of the
loyalty that we feel towards them. And this is not just a piece of
ideological deception; it derives from the recognition that my
individuality is itself a social product and the product not of
society in the abstract, but of the specific society in which I live.
The answer that I should help 'A' rather than 'B' because 'A' is
'one of us' may express a coldly rational calculation, but it is
more likely to express a pre-rational feeling: 'A' is a member of
our group; naturally, we feel more regard for him than we do for
outsiders.

We are just, then, because justice keeps society going—not
society in general but our society—and that is necessary for us.
But one of the main themes of this book is that the rise of the
disengaged view is undermining this association with society.
An individual is a social being, but he is also—an individual. As
he becomes more conscious of this, his sense of belonging to an
'organic' community—whether defined by race, religion, or
class—tends to break down. This may lead to the development
of a more general sense of justice, one that embraces everyone,
not just the members of one's community (compare Aristotle
with the Stoics here)—or it may lead to a purely amoral individualism, in which the individual refuses to acknowledge
obligations to anyone (except perhaps to other individuals for
whom he cares), unless forced to do so by the power of the law.
In so far as justice involves a sense of belonging to a community
of equals admitting mutual claims of right, it is threatened by
the breakdown of the sense of community that comes with the

rise of the disengaged ideal. It may be said that, when philosophers from Socrates to Philippa Foot ask themselves why an individual should act justly, and try to show what is in it for him if he does, that this presupposes a state of social disintegration. In an 'organic' society a person does not think of himself as an individual first, and then try to see what benefit he would gain from participating in society; he thinks of himself as a member of the community, and does not try to play off his own interests against those of his fellows. But, as I have said before, the very fact that people do ask why they should be just means that the organic society has broken down, and it is rather ironic that conservative theorists should hope to restore it by rational arguments in favour of an organic community. In a society with a developed sense of individuality, the question: Why be just? Why pursue another person's good, or be unwilling to sacrifice it to my own good?—becomes a genuine and rather pressing one. This suggests that Judge William's advice to the disengaged aesthete to 'repent himself back' into the life of his community is not going to be so easy to follow as he seems to imply. (A point that Kierkegaard himself makes in his social criticism, which I discuss below.)

Some rather similar points can be made about another social (or civic) virtue: benevolence. This does not appear in the classical lists of the virtues, and—as it features in our modern Western tradition—is no doubt a secularized version of the Christian virtue of *agape*. However, I think it can be seen to be a virtue without presupposing any particular religious background. A society in which people are not only just, but are actively concerned for one another's well-being, is a more pleasant society to live in than one in which people are only just. Justice without benevolence is a somewhat cold virtue. Various modern ethical writers—from Hume and Schopenhauer, in their different ways, to Richard Taylor (amongst others) today—have tried to make benevolence or sympathy the key concept in ethics. There is something right here. Schopenhauer has a thought-experiment. Two men are planning murders; they are confident that they will not be detected. But they decide not to carry out their plans. One is allowed to give any of the arguments that moral philosophers have come up with as his reason for desisting from the murder (Schopenhauer refers to the reasons that would be given by Kant, Fichte, Hutchinson, Adam Smith, and Spinoza, amongst others); the second man says simply 'I was . . . seized with pity and compassion; I felt sorry for him; I had not the heart to do it, and could not.'[66] Schopenhauer now asks us: 'Which of the two is the better man? . . . Which of them was restrained by the purer motive?'[67] Surely it is true that most of the kind and unselfish behaviour that there is in the world is simply the outcome of sympathy or benevolence—a feeling that is, to some extent, natural to us. (As Mencius remarks: 'if, for instance, a child is suddenly seen to be on the point of falling into a well, everybody without exception will have a sense of distress. It is not by reason of any close intimacy with the parent of the child, nor by reason of a desire for the praise of neighbours and friends . . .'[68])

However, this approach soon runs into difficulties. If benevolence is treated simply as a feeling, then some people have it and some do not. And to those that do not, what more can be said, except threateningly? If benevolence is to be considered a virtue, a disposition to be developed and cultivated, it would seem that it should be possible to give some reason why such an—often awkward—disposition should be cherished. It is all very well for Foot to say that we should think of ourselves 'as volunteers banded together to fight for liberty and justice, and against inhumanity and oppression', rather than as conscripts press-ganged by the Categorical Imperative.[69] But it is worth remembering how many volunteers have been persuaded to go forward to be killed or maimed for causes that have no significance for their own lives at all. When, as a disengaged individual, I reflect on why I should cultivate a disposition that may cause me great pain, great inconvenience, force me to abandon plans and projects of great significance to me, and even, perhaps, lead to my torture and death, it might seem that quite a good answer would be needed. To be sure, there is every reason why I should want others to be benevolent; there is good reason why I should try to inculcate that virtue in my children.

---

[66] A. Schopenhauer, *On the Basis of Morality*, trans. E. F. J. Payne (Indianapolis, 1965), 169.   [67] Ibid.

[68] E. R. Hughes (ed.), *Chinese Philosophy in Classical Times* (London, 1954), 101.

[69] P. Foot, 'Morality as a System of Hypothetical Imperatives', in her *Virtues and Vices*, 167.

But reflecting on that fact should lead me to wonder about the extent to which my 'natural feelings' of sympathy were implanted in me, or at least nurtured by my educators for their good and the good of society at large, rather than for my own good. And—despite perfectly valid objections to the 'genetic fallacy'—to reflect on 'the genealogy of morals' has a tendency to undermine the present force of moral requirements and demands.

To this line of thought, we can reply (in, I believe, the spirit of Judge William) that to think in such a way is to adopt an individualistic stance which cannot prove ultimately satisfying. Disengagement ends in despair. Because the individual is also a social self, and remains so even in his capacity to transcend the social or in his alienation from it, he cannot fully satisfy himself in a state of complete disengagement, of spiritual exile from the rest of the human race. To accept one's social identity means to become vulnerable, to take the risks involved in caring for other people, but only in this way is it possible to enjoy the satisfaction of belonging to a community, of reciprocal concern, of shared joy, and shared sorrow also. Jonathan Bennett ends a paper that argues for the maintenance of a sharp sense of compassion as a safeguard against inhuman moral principles by quoting from Wilfred Owen's 'Insensibility'. The poem is about those who have numbed their sensibilities, and thus avoid the pain of compassionate suffering. Bennett remarks that, despite this, for Owen, 'they are the losers, because they have cut themselves off from the human condition', and he quotes:

> By choice they made themselves immune
> To pity and whatever moans in man
> Before the last sea and the hapless stars;
> Whatever mourns when many leave those shores;
> Whatever shares
> The eternal reciprocity of tears.[70]

However, one could reply to this, as I said earlier when discussing justice, that membership of, and identification with, one group is not something that can necessarily lead to a universal extension of attitudes. I may feel deep concern and benevolence for my family, my friends, perhaps even for my

---

[70] J. Bennett, 'The Conscience of Huckleberry Finn', *Philosophy* (1974), 134.

countrymen or co-religionists, but this may not extend beyond these circles, any more than I need to feel that I should behave justly to those outside my community. Mackie dismisses utilitarianism—and the biblical injunction to love one's neighbour as oneself—as 'the ethics of fantasy'.[71] Williams makes a rather similar protest at the—Kantian as well as utilitarian—idea that we should be equally concerned for all people, that we should feel a universal benevolence. How can I be said to love someone, if I feel no more concerned for him than for anyone else?[72] I may well feel a generalized goodwill towards people, but this only hardens into the active concern that may impel me to make serious sacrifices for others with regard to comparatively few people. I can certainly see no reason, other than a religious one, for extending this concern beyond the immediate circle of those who are close to me.

Whatever projects one undertakes, one will need the virtues of courage, self-control, and practical wisdom, and also the virtue of honest perception which I mentioned above. In so far as one is committed to living in society—and I have argued that one cannot really avoid so doing—one will also need the virtues of justice and benevolence, in some measure anyway. Now, a virtue is a disposition: if I have developed the virtue of courage, I can be said to be a brave man, and this is so with the other virtues. Thus they give a constancy and stability to my character. Someone who possesses the virtues is one who can be relied upon to be brave, just, prudent. He can be depended on—unlike the aesthete, who may be able to act bravely or justly on occasion, but who has no constant disposition to do so. The more spontaneously and unreflectively I take the courageous or the benevolent course of action, the more I can be said to possess the relevant virtue. It is acquired, however, by a process of self-discipline, and, in this, is unlike the 'aesthetic seriousness' that Judge William discusses briefly,[73] and which consists in

---

[71] J. L. Mackie, *Ethics: Inventing Right and Wrong* (Harmondsworth, 1977), 130–1.

[72] See also S. Freud, *Civilisation and its Discontents*, trans. J. Strachey (New York and London,, 1961), 62 ff., where he says of the commandment to love one's neighbour as oneself: 'Let us adopt a naive attitude towards it . . . Why should we do it? What good will it do us? But, above all, how shall we achieve it? How can it be possible? My love is something valuable to me which I ought not to throw away without reflection.'   [73] *E/O* ii. 265.

concentrating on the development of one particular ability or talent. Of course, courage, benevolence, self-control come more easily to some than to others. But the ethical task of developing the virtues is the same for everyone, whatever the initial psychological material that one has to work with. This is quite different from the aesthetic seriousness, which perhaps cultivates one particular disposition just because it seems to be the strongest that the person has. Whether or not it comes easily to me, it is still the ethical task for me to develop the virtue of courage; I cannot shrug it off by just saying that I am a cowardly sort of person—as I could shrug off a demand that I develop my musical talents by saying that I am just not musical.

The need to cultivate the virtues derives from the need to engage in projects, and this derives from the need to live a coherent and meaningful life. But what projects should one adopt? I have argued that the 'personal' virtues are necessary to any project, and that the 'civic' virtues are necessary to any project that involves social co-operation. So we can make some considerable progress towards developing a coherent ethic without specifying what projects people should adopt (except for the minimal point that we assume that they will involve some social element). This is a quite Kierkegaardian conclusion: Judge William is constantly admonishing 'A' not so much to commit himself to some *particular* thing, as to commit himself to *something*, just to avoid wholly volatilizing his soul. But is this enough? Surely one can commit oneself to evil projects. Is there anything we have said so far that rules this out?

What if someone becomes a Nazi—and he may be someone who has been influenced by existentialism, and is looking for something to which to commit himself, a project that will give his life meaning (I do not doubt that this was actually part of the appeal of Nazism in the disordered and demoralized Germany of the early 1930s). Now, in taking on the task of becoming a good Nazi, he may well develop all the virtues that I have mentioned—including justice and compassion towards his fellow Nazis. He would also be brave, self-controlled, efficient, and so on. His life has meaning, has purpose; he is working as part of a wider community; there is a narrative structure to his life, a stability, constancy, and continuity in his character. So what is wrong? Some existentialist philosophers would say that there is nothing more that philosophy can say on this point, though we may choose to commit ourselves to anti-Nazi positions, and simply oppose our Nazi. (One great existentialist philosopher became notorious for saying that nothing was wrong at all, that such a commitment to Nazism was right and splendid.) Is this the necessary upshot of Kierkegaard's dictum that 'The objective accent falls on WHAT is said, the subjective accent on HOW it is said'?[74] Or is there some way in which we can choose between projects and condemn some? If not, it may seem that the Kierkegaardian position is an irrationalist one after all.

The problem is one that Judge William does not seem to notice. As he sees it, 'A' can choose between frittering away his life as he is doing, or joining the civic, social, and religious life of his community; taking a job, marrying and raising a family, attending the services of the established Church. But there are other projects—and I think that our Nazi (and here I am distinguishing him from the time-servers, thugs, opportunists, and crowd men who doubtless made up most of the Nazi ranks) is genuinely pursuing a project, as opposed to someone like Johannes the Seducer, who is certainly dedicated to his favoured way of life, but only with 'aesthetic seriousness'. I think that we are coming up against the limits of the purely ethical sphere of existence here. We can see that some virtues are necessary for any project. We can also see that other virtues are necessary for any social projects, and are therefore, in effect, unavoidable, though we have not yet found any convincing justification for universal compassion or even universal justice. Furthermore, we can say that any particular project will have its own standards of success or failure; so long as I consider that project to be significant for me, so long as I think of myself *as* a scientist or an engineer or an officer or whatever, then to fail in so being, to do badly at those things as judged by the standard public criteria for success, is in part to fail as a person. (An officer who shoots himself because he has failed to live up to the code of military ethics certainly sees things in this way.) But is there any way in which we can assess projects themselves as good or bad?

[74] *CUP* 181.

To some extent, we have already been doing so in arguing for the necessity of the social virtues. In asserting that some social involvement is part of the good life, I was moving the argument to a more explicitly teleological level, and starting to sketch out what the good life for man might look like. And one can take the process further, though an account of which projects are fulfilling will never be free from controversy. Still, one might start by claiming that love, friendship, and creativity of one sort or another are good projects to pursue; there may not be too much controversy here. And each of these projects requires its own distinctive virtues to be cultivated. But, though there can be broad agreement among people of very different world-views as to some projects that can be regarded as good, before we have gone very far we will start to encounter important divergences. And it is at this level of general world-view that we must look for general criteria for the assessment of projects. We are thus brought to the question of the relation between the ethical and the religious, which is the subject of my concluding chapter.

3.2.5. *Jesus, Parfit, Wittgenstein, and the Buddha*

Before I go on to these questions, however, there remains an objection to what I have said so far which needs to be discussed. I have tried to argue up to this point that we do desire to establish a coherent personal identity across time. But many religious and ethical teachings have presented it as the highest good not to create or build up a self, but to break it down, to escape from the prison of selfhood. For the Buddhist, the idea of an enduring self is one of the great illusions from which we must free ourselves. The New Testament tells us to break with our pasts by being reborn, while learning also to take no care for the future: 'Sufficient unto the day *is* the evil thereof.'[75] Wittgenstein writes that 'the man is fulfilling the purpose of existence who no longer needs to have any purpose except to live'.[76] And again: 'Only a man who lives not in time but in the present is happy.'[77] Parfit, who alludes to the Buddhist doctrine of *an-atta*—no self—in support of his own claim that there is no

---

[75] Matthew 6: 34.
[76] L. Wittgenstein, *Notebooks, 1914–1916*, trans. G. E. M. Anscombe (Oxford, 1961), 73 (6 July 1916).   [77] Ibid. 74 (8 July 1916).

'deep fact' about personal identity, says that this realization is 'liberating and consoling'. He no longer feels that he is moving through a 'glass tunnel', essentially isolated from others. 'I now live in the open air . . . I am less concerned about the rest of my own life and more concerned about the lives of others.'[78]

To these objections, I would reply, first, that the ethic that I have outlined is a deliberately non-metaphysical one. It takes human nature much as it finds it, and does not raise large questions about the ultimate value or disvalue of existence. Instead, it tries to suggest how a reasonably satisfactory life can be led without answering—or, indeed, asking—such questions. The ethicist disciplines and orders his desires, whereas the aesthete does not. But a Buddhist would rightly observe that his life is still full of desire and directed to the satisfaction of desire—and thus, according to Buddhism as I understand it, it is still a life doomed to continual suffering and frustration. To live like a bourgeois rather than a bohemian is to exchange one type of worldly life for another; Buddism, though, is a radical negation of all such worldliness. What it recommends is a withdrawal, a detachment, from life itself. This may be right; but then Buddhism involves a repudiation of the ethical in my sense. In this case it is not a direct threat to what I have been saying: a Buddhist may hypothetically agree that, if life in samsara were worth living, it would be as the ethicist lives it; it is just that he denies the hypothetical premiss, and prefers to go in search of nirvana.

It is worth noting, though, that someone who wishes to lead the life of a good Buddhist, and thereby to attain nirvana, has adopted a peculiarly rigorous project. He must develop the virtues, including universal compassion and various specifically ascetic ones, concern himself with the progress of his spiritual development through time, and so on. And if he has any measure of success, he will build up a formidably concentrated and disciplined personality. All this is a means to the end, no doubt, a ladder to be kicked away; but the seriously undertaken rejection of life is itself a project, and one that may be sufficiently absorbing to give meaning to many lives.

Christian ethics is not so much ascetic as eschatological in

[78] Parfit, *Reasons and Persons*, 281.

nature, but that is a topic for the next chapter. As for Wittgenstein, he makes a sharp distinction between the pure I— the disengaged knowing subject, the 'limit of the world'—and the ordinary empirical self. He explicitly says that the pure I is no closer to 'its' empirical personality than to any other person—or, indeed, thing—in the world.[79] That is why it can be 'content' whatever happens; surveying the world without identifying with any of its contents, the pure I enjoys the 'life of knowledge' which is secure from the 'miseries of the world'.[80] But we have here a dualism so radical as to amount to a form of metaphysical schizophrenia. It is all very well for the pure self to be timeless and detached, but how does this help me—the messy, struggling, empirical person who has to live in time? As Schopenhauer realized, moments of pure aesthetic contemplation may seem to lift us out of time and out of our daily struggles, but they soon pass, and we are left once again wondering where the next meal is to come from.

At first sight, Parfit's hostility to the maintenance of personal identity through time does not seem to depend on an appeal to such back-stage entities as nirvana, the kingdom of God, or the metaphysical I. But he wavers between asserting that there really is no such thing as enduring personhood—it is just a fundamental metaphysical fact that I am simply a series of short-term selves—and the more Kierkegaardian view that a person may be more or less of a self—personal identity is something that we can either make or not make. On the first interpretation, we can—although it is very difficult—find liberation and enlightenment in accepting the fact of our irremediable discontinuity. On the second interpretation, Parfit's philosophy becomes a moral injunction to us not to become selves, to refrain from developing a personal identity and, by so doing, imprisoning ourselves each in his separate 'glass tunnel'. Should this injunction be heeded? Parfit thinks that if we become less concerned for our futures, we should become more concerned for other people. He writes that, on his view, 'There is still a difference between my life and the lives of other people. But the difference is less. Other people are closer.'[81]

[79] Wittgenstein, *Notebooks, 1914–1916*, 82 (2 Sept. 1916).
[80] Ibid. 81 (13 Aug. 1916).   [81] Parfit, *Reasons and Persons*, 281.

I do not see that this follows at all. My life has at least the continuity of the life of a physical organism, in any case. And there remains the difference between the organism that is me, and those that are others. That difference is bridged by my entering into personal relationships with others. But, if these are at all serious, they continue over a period of time, develop their own history and continuity, and demand of me the fostering of certain virtues and a certain stability of character, without which friendship and love are not possible. The memories that I share with others, our plans together for the future, tie us together in the present; and it is these things that give my life its continuity, keep it from disintegrating into a succession of short-term selves. If my life does so fall apart as to lack substantial continuity, then I really would be shut off from others—as Kierkegaard's aesthetes are—intensely egotistical, but lacking selves. Continuity in one's own life, and the capacity to enter into relationships with others, are the two sides of one coin. Parfit hopes to make way for general altruism by deconstructing the idea of the continuing self, but it would seem that a short-term self would have little reason to care about either his successors or any other selves. Parfit does worry about this,[82] but not as much as I think he should. The ethic suggested by his views on personal identity seems to be not utilitarianism, but an egoistic hedonism of the present moment. And I think Kierkegaard is psychologically right here; such a life issues in despair, and this despair comes about through a sense of the lack of coherence in one's life. This suggests that the attainment of continuity is part of our *telos*, of the good life for us—which is not, of course, to deny that there is value in spontaneity.

[82] Parfit, *Reasons and Persons*, §102, pp. 307–12.

4

FROM ETHICS TO RELIGION

4.1. LIMITATIONS OF THE ETHICAL

So far I have attempted sympathetically to reconstruct Kierke-gaard's argument for the ethical. I think that this argument shows that there is good reason for making serious commitments to certain ground projects, which involves accepting the conventional, intersubjective standards of assessment that go with such projects. I have also argued for the necessity of cultivating certain virtues which are generally valuable for the carrying-out of whatever projects one has adopted. Finally, I argued that there is reason to believe that there can be some consensus as to which projects are good and worth pursuing, though the amount of agreement likely to emerge here should not be overestimated.

I have not, however, provided any justification for universal benevolence or justice. And, given a purely naturalistic account of human nature, I do not see that we can discover, in any sense that would be important for ethics, a human essence by reference to which we could determine what constitutes the uniquely good life for any human being. In this case, we are left with a plurality of goods, of goals that we pursue, and no agreed way of ordering them, or of finding more than a rather limited degree of agreement as to which of these goods which people pursue really are goods. So, my interpretation of Kierkegaard thus far does not provide much support for 'morality' as the 'core meaning' of that concept is expounded by Alan Gewirth:

a morality is a set of categorically obligatory requirements for action that are addressed, at least in part, to every actual or prospective agent, and that are concerned with furthering the interests, especially the most important interests, of persons or recipients other than, or in addition to the agent or speaker. The requirements are . . . mandatory for the conduct of every person to whom they are addressed . . .

although one moral requirement may be overridden by another, it may not be overridden by any non-moral requirement, nor can its normative bindingness be escaped by shifting one's inclinations, opinions or ideals.[1]

The substantive philosophical point that I want to make in this chapter is that such a conception of morality can only be vindicated on religious premises; and that, accordingly—and contrary to the opinions of many philosophers—someone's religious beliefs or disbeliefs will make an important difference to his or her moral beliefs. However, I also want to show, again by a sympathetic reconstruction of Kierkegaard's arguments, that there is a rationale for religious commitment which is analogous to, and, indeed, an extension of, the rationale for ethical commitment which I have just outlined. 'The heart has its reasons',[2] and it is these that lead to religious faith, but Pascal exaggerates when he says that reason can know nothing of them. Kierkegaard's—and, for that matter, Pascal's—psychological writings are attempts to give some account of the factors that incline the existentially concerned individual to faith.

I want to start by discussing Kierkegaard's reasons for finding the purely ethical sphere unsatisfactory. It should be noted that Kierkegaard himself thought of the ethical as having a religious aspect; Judge William thinks of himself as a religious man. I do not believe that the religious element is essential to the Judge's thought, hence its omission from the previous chapter, but it does mean that Kierkegaard did not have much to say specifically in criticism of an atheistic, secular approach to ethics. Rather, he starts from the existing religious consciousness within the ethical, which typically assumes that we relate to God mainly by the simple performance of our social duties. Starting from their own professions of religious belief, Kierkegaard aims to show those at the ethical level that religion makes greater demands than they have been willing to acknowledge. This presents them with a dilemma: they must either stay at the level of social morality, and accept that they are not religious in any decisive sense, or they must move to a more seriously religious level. This is the argument that is presented most impressively in *Fear and Trembling*, which I shall discuss in some detail later.

---

[1] A. Gewirth, *Reason and Morality* (Chicago and London, 1978), 1.

[2] B. Pascal, *Pensées*, trans. A. J. Krailsheimer (Harmondsworth, 1986), §423.

For the moment, though, I want to examine some factors that might lead a secular moralist without any religious preconceptions to adopt a religious stance. In so doing, I shall continue to draw on Kierkegaard's arguments, though I shall be transposing them into a somewhat different framework. The point of my discussion will be to clarify further the nature and limits of the ethics that I developed in Chapter 3. One may then choose to affirm the purely ethical, accepting those limitations, or choose to go beyond it, in the hope of reaching past those limits.

In what follows, I shall be drawing on a number of Kierkegaard's works in order to bring out the limitations of the ethical as a self-enclosed sphere. I shall concentrate on three points: (i) the inability of a social morality to do justice to the uniqueness of each individual; (ii) the erosion, in the modern world, of the social basis for a morality of conformity to customary roles; and (iii) the pluralism of a secular ethics, its lack of a single goal in striving towards which the moral life finds its unity. These three points are closely connected, making it impossible to treat any of them in complete isolation from the others.

4.1.1. *The Individual*

Kierkegaard is, of course, notorious for his individualism. In *Either/Or* he has Judge William arguing for an ethic of social conformity, but more typical of Kierkegaard—what we think of as most deeply Kierkegaardian—is the passionate call for individual responsibility. Each one of us must work out his own salvation in fear and trembling; each of us is accountable for his own actions—God will not be impressed by the excuse that the evil we did was sanctioned by the social norms of our day.

A man might very well live his entire life, be married, become known and respected as citizen, father and captain of the hunt, without ever having discovered God in His works, and without ever having received any impression of the infinitude of the ethical because . . . he helped himself out by having recourse to the customs and traditions prevailing in the town where he happened to live. As a mother admonishes her child when it sets off for a party, 'Now, be sure to behave yourself, and do as you see the other well-behaved children do'—so he might manage to live by conducting himself as he sees others do.[3]

[3] *CUP* 218.

Each man himself, as an individual, should render his account to God
. . . the most ruinous evasion of all is to be hidden in the crowd in an
attempt to escape God's supervision of him as an individual . . .
eternity will demand of him that he shall have lived as an individual.[4]

This is the existentialist Kierkegaard, the spokesman for the
free, lonely, responsible individual, whose voice, taken up and
amplified by so many, from Ibsen through Sartre to the present
day, has resonated so powerfully in our culture. What has
largely been put aside has been the religious background to that
individualism, which is so strongly emphasized in the quotations
above. But, for Kierkegaard, this background is crucial. For on
what basis does the individual decide that he cannot go along
with the conventions of his society? If it is simply that he feels
them to be irksome, this is a lapse back into aestheticism. If the
objection is an ethical one, what foundations can there be for it?
There is no particular problem about piecemeal moral reform—
someone may try to draw out more rigorously the consequences
of principles accepted in his society, to overcome conflicts
between rival recognized values and so on—but on what basis
can someone criticize the customs of his society as a whole?
What basis can he have for standing back from the crowd, for
believing that he has duties as an individual which may or may
not be in conflict with his social duties, but which cannot,
anyway, be subsumed under them? The only answer, if we
reject the Kantian style of moral philosophy as illusion, is that
the individual has decided that the customs of his society are not
such as to further the pursuit of the good life for man.

To make such a judgement, he does not need to have any very
clear conception of what is good himself; he may decide that the
social customs to which he objects depend on beliefs, perhaps
religious beliefs, that he deems to be false. But if he has no
alternative conception of the good to which he can give his
allegiance, once he has rejected that which is embodied in the
social practices of his community, then, again, he lapses back
into aestheticism, with all its attendant disadvantages. Now, the
vision of the good life to which an individual may adhere and on
the basis of which he rejects or, at least, supplements that of his
society, need not be religious. He may be an Epicurean or a

[4] *P of H* 162–3.

Benthamite or a Marxist. But the problem is that any claim to have discovered an essence of human nature, one that 'timelessly demanded a life of a particular kind',[5] simply by using the methods of naturalistic psychology and anthropology, tends to look pretty implausible. If we have an account of human nature that is much more sophisticated than the infantile psychology of Benthamite utilitarianism, then it seems too complex to yield any clear conception of the good, one against which I can measure the shortcomings of my society.

The question of how the individual can mount a critique of his society is addressed by Sabina Lovibond in her book *Realism and Imagination in Ethics*. There she argues for an understanding of ethics akin to Hegel's *Sittlichkeit*. Her approach is to draw on Wittgenstein's philosophy of language for an account of morality as a form of life into which we are initiated by being trained to recognize intersubjectively valid standards of judgement; by, in the first place, submitting to 'intellectual authority relations'. She is then faced with the problem that this seems to justify a very conservative stance, one in which the individual is left with no ground to stand on if he attempts to judge his society morally, for the intelligibility of his moral discourse depends on his participation in social practices. Attempting to get round this, she argues that the individual can choose to distance himself from the moral institutions of his society; we can use its moral concepts 'only in so far as we can "find ourselves" in the specific repertoire of social practices which happen, historically, to "lie at the bottom" of evaluative discourse within the community to which we belong'. And this can be done only when 'an expressive relation can be said to exist between these practices and ourselves'.[6]

Thus, as in *Either/Or*, the disengaged individual does not have 'concepts of unconditional value . . . available for [his] (non-ironic) use', unless he participates in the moral practices of his community. But this only makes it harder to see how there can be a radical moral critique of the prevailing *Sittlichkeit*. Lovibond worries (with some reference to Bradley) whether this neo-Hegelian approach to ethics must ultimately lead one to conclude 'that rational dissent from the prevailing consensual

[5] B. Williams, *Ethics and the Limits of Philosophy* (London, 1985), 153.
[6] S. Lovibond, *Realism and Imagination in Ethics* (Oxford, 1983), 89.

world-view [is] a logical impossibility'.[7] In opposing this extreme view, she points out that a society's moral standards do not comprise a monolithic unity—there are different, related moral language games rather than just one; nor do we demand the same degree of uniformity in morals as in mathematics. So 'in a community where intellectual cohesion exists only in a low degree, there will be nothing to prevent individual members from rationalising their distaste for a particular sub-set of the prevailing values (or institutions) in terms of an alternative or divergent scheme of values, through which they can sustain their identity as rational persons . . .'[8]

As an account of how piecemeal moral criticism is possible, this is fine. But we can now confront Lovibond with a dilemma. Either the dissident's scheme of values is radically divergent from that of the community as a whole, or it is not. If not, it may be the basis for a reformist stance, but not for a genuinely radical critique. If it is, then adherence to such a scheme lifts the dissident altogether outside 'his' community. Perhaps these values will still be embodied in the life of some social group, be it an oppressed class or a religious sect, but if its values diverge radically from those of society as a whole, it ceases to be a subgroup of that wider whole, and becomes just another group, the two groups and their rival schemes of values simply confronting one another, each one internally unified. A society, in other words, does not need to be monolithic. It can include various groups with differing outlooks. But if these outlooks are radically different, then we do not have a single society at all, but several different ones, each with its own set of values. And this does nothing to explain how the individual can mount a moral critique of the society in which he finds himself, *qua* individual and not just *qua* member of some other group, constrained to live, for whatever reasons, *in partibus infidelium*.

Kierkegaard's individualism—the insistence that each of us must judge for him- or herself, and not blindly follow social convention—strikes a chord with most of us. But, unless this is to be a return to aestheticism, with all the weaknesses that we have diagnosed in that position, it seems that this individualism must be able to appeal to higher standards of behaviour than

[7] S. Lovibond, *Realism and Imagination in Ethics* (Oxford, 1983), 109.
[8] Ibid. 127–8.

those of society. And the most obvious candidates for such standards are religious ones. There remains the possibility of appealing beyond social convention to the commitments arising from personal relationships. But if these are without any conventional, institutional backing, it may be hard (not impossible) to distinguish a serious commitment to a ground project from a temporary aesthetic mood. For every Gauguin who abandons his family and goes to Tahiti out of dedication to his art, there are doubtless many more 'Gauguins' who do the same, claiming to themselves and others that they have the same motives, but who are in fact aesthetes (in the Kierkegaardian sense) off to Tahiti because it is more fun than caring for their families. Of course, similar points could be made about those who claim to have religious grounds for transcending the conventions of society. (Kierkegaard was well aware of this.) This is the anguish of the post-conventional moralist, whether religious or not; in refusing simply to take his standards of good and evil from his society, is he really performing a 'teleological suspension of the ethical'—that is acting for the sake of realizing a higher *telos* than the social one—or is he lapsing back into an aestheticism that is not even honest, as it conceals its true, self-indulgent motives with high-flown talk of self-realization? Abraham can never be sure whether he is obeying the commands of God, or giving in to the temptations of the Devil.[9]

I will say more about Abraham's predicament later. Kierkegaard does not have much to say about the possibility of a non-religious transcendence of the ethical. I suspect that he would have regarded it as a mere reversion to aestheticism—'aesthetic seriousness', at best—whatever the fancy rhetoric. However, although the mature ethicist is no mere crowd man, and although his arguments against the aesthete are good, there remains a sense in which, from Kierkegaard's own perspective, the debate between them does end in stalemate. For the aesthete, in his individualism and his scepticism about the possibility of finding real fulfilment in the rather complacent conventionalism of Judge William, has some conception of real and important values that are beyond the Judge's ken. For Kierkegaard, individuality and self-formative commitment to

[9] Cf. *FT* 79.

projects can only be held together at the religious level. The aesthete neglects the latter, and his soul is dissipated in multiplicity. The ethicist neglects the former, and he vanishes into the mass of the conventionally respectable. Only the religious man can combine the two in his life.

According to Kierkegaard himself, then, Judge William's ethic of conformity to social standards fails to do justice to the value of individuality. I have argued that there is some truth in this criticism, but, nevertheless, Kierkegaard's individualism has been attacked—with some initial plausibility—as exaggerated and one-sided. The following section will examine this criticism, and aim to show in response to it that Kierkegaard's account of the relationship between the individual and his society is a good deal more subtle and careful than is often recognized. His passionate individualism coexists with a sense of the importance of social values. However, in his social criticism—contained principally in *Two Ages*, but also in *Works of Love* and in the *Journals*—he advances an argument that some kind of disengaged individualism is being forced upon us by the way in which our society is developing; the 'organic' community, which is the natural setting for Judge William's social ethics, is disappearing, and, as a result, the morality of social roles is fast becoming an anachronism.

4.1.2. The Individual and the Crowd

Kierkegaard's stress on the free, solitary individual, his contempt for the sheep-like behaviour of 'the crowd', make it easy to read him as a purely asocial thinker, a radical individualist who rejects all social values. Marjorie Greene claims that, for him, 'turning to inwardness necessarily means turning to the self as totally isolated from other selves [and] . . . completely away from any conception of human community.'[10] Janik and Toulmin agree: 'Kierkegaard . . . maintained that true morality is asocial, because it consists in an absolutely immediate relationship between each man and God . . . In this relationship the friend or fellow-man becomes the unnecessary other.'[11] If this is correct, then Kierkegaard is exposed to the extremely

---

[10] M. Greene, *Introduction to Existentialism* (Chicago, 1959), 39.
[11] A. Janik and S. Toulmin, *Wittgenstein's Vienna* (New York, 1973), 157.

damaging criticism that he 'abstracted the self from society as violently as any speculative philosopher ever abstracted the life of reason from his existence as a man'.[12] The criticism is that, for all his stress on the concrete realities of existence, Kierkegaard actually presents us with an unreal—because abstract—account of the self; one that takes no heed of a person's relation to social reality. And Marxist critics, of course, have seen this abstraction as an ideological reflection of the atomized individualism of bourgeois society. With specific reference to Kierkegaard, Adorno writes: 'Genuineness is nothing other than a defiant and obstinate insistence on the monadological form which social oppression imposes on man.'[13]

I certainly do not want to claim that there is nothing in these criticisms. But Kierkegaard's position is, nevertheless, more defensible than those who make them seem to realize. A reading of *Works of Love* is enough to refute the claim that his ethic is 'asocial'. Kierkegaard's own temperament and his polemical concerns did tug him towards an extreme individualism at times, but much more positive evaluations of human society can be found in his works if we look for them. As for the Marxist criticism, Kierkegaard was as concerned as Adorno to work out a vision of non-alienated human relationships; while Adorno, in his condemnation of all existing forms of society, ends up in a position at least as individualistic as Kierkegaard's; the lonely critical theorist, with his superior knowledge, must stand aloof from corrupt society, and especially from the masses, consumers of the 'culture industry'. With regard to the charge that his individualism is merely 'bourgeois', Kierkegaard could reply that he is well aware of the social changes taking place in his day, and is concerned to understand contemporary individualism and its ethical significance, rather than to launch simplistic polemics *pro* or *contra*.

For all his mockery of Hegel's world-historical pretensions, Kierkegaard himself suggests a schematic view of the evolution of (Western) society.

The dialectic of antiquity was oriented to the eminent (the great individual—and then the crowd; one free man, and then the slaves); at

---

[12] H. R. Niebuhr, *Christ and Culture* (New York, 1951), 243.
[13] T. W. Adorno, *Minima moralia*, trans. E. Jephcott (London, 1976), 154.

present, the dialectic of Christianity is oriented to representation (the majority perceive themselves in the representative and are liberated by the awareness that he is representing them in a kind of self-consciousness). The dialectic of the present age is oriented to equality, and its most logical implementation, albeit abortive, is levelling, the negative unity of the negative mutual reciprocity of individuals.[14]

This passage is at once dense and sketchy, but it suggests some interesting ideas. In classical antiquity—and, one might suggest, in some more recent civilizations—there is no sense of fundamental human equality. Men and women, nobles and commoners, freemen and slaves, ruler and subjects existed in strictly hierarchical relationships; there is no sense of a basic equality, a common humanity. The ruler, the 'eminent individual', considered himself qualitatively superior to the mass of the people; they existed as means to the end of his glory. Christianity changes that, with its stress on the equality of all people before God. This does not lead directly to socio-political change, but it does bring about a revolution in attitude. In so far as they have been genuinely affected by Christian ideals, rulers and nobles know that there is no qualitative difference between themselves and the poorest of the poor. Of course, they possess advantages and privileges, but their temporal power is a stewardship, granted to them by God, and they are answerable to God for their use of it. The poor remain poor, but they are not spiritually crushed by this poverty; they know that it is not a mark of their intrinsic inferiority as human beings. Kierkegaard characterizes this stage as one of 'representation'. Hannay thinks that he means by this 'the "democratic" system as we know it',[15] but this is surely wrong; such a system did not exist in the Denmark of 1846, nor could it be found in any very developed form elsewhere in Europe before that time. Democracy as we know it was one of the social changes that Kierkegaard saw coming with very mixed feelings. The 'representative' phase is that of the society mentioned above; hierarchical, but infused with Christian ideals. It is representative in the sense that its people understand the need for hierarchy, for social and political inequality, but do not see this as contradicting the essential equality of all people before God. So, someone must

---

[14] *TA* 84.   [15] A. Hannay, *Kierkegaard* (London, 1982), 280.

rule, but not because he is a superior individual; on the contrary, he is just one of us—and therefore 'representative'. He has no spiritual eminence, but is marked out in a purely functional manner as king or ruler because someone must rule, there must be structures of authority in any society. 'Therefore the king is no incarnation, not a being we should worship; he is a weak, fragile human being like the rest of us, but he is king by the grace of God and it is this religious boundary which limits and terminates the state.'[16]

This state of affairs is one that Kierkegaard admires and sympathizes with. Society is 'organic'; the individual recognizes his place within the larger whole of the social organism, without this recognition—as in antiquity—crushing his individuality; that is protected by his knowledge of his individual relationship to God, in which social status is of no importance. But in political life it is important; the lower classes should submit cheerfully to authority, while those who wield it should do so responsibly and not for the sake of personal gain. What Kierkegaard presents here is a roughly Burkean conservativism. Human beings naturally and unreflectively accept their social roles in a stratified, hierarchical society, without being either humiliated by a lowly role or puffed up by an eminent one. Kierkegaard's admiration for this order is brought out in an interesting way by his opposition to feminism. He is horrified by antiquity's contempt for woman, when 'she, almost an animal, was a contemptible being in comparison with the man'.[17] Christianity has changed this, but it 'brings about only the change of the infinite and therefore in all stillness. The external remains in a manner the old; for the man must be the woman's lord, she submissive to him . . .'[18] In general, Kierkegaard admires a 'Christian' order in which the social structures of antiquity remain at least largely unchanged, but the form that they provide for society is filled with a new content—that of Christian love. Christianity

has not taken away the differences in the earthly life. These must continue as long as the temporal existence continues, and must continue to tempt every man who comes into the world. For by being a

[16] *Journals* 4097.   [17] *W of L* 112.   [18] Ibid.

Christian, he is not exempt from the differences, but by triumphing over the temptation of the differences, he becomes Christian.[19]

The earthly difference is always a temptation. Alas! Perhaps it does more than tempt, so that one man becomes arrogant, the other defiantly envious. Both cases are rebellious, rebellious against the Christian.[20]

I have called Kierkegaard's vision of society 'Burkean', but it is distinguished from conventional conservativism, for Kierkegaard accepts that the organic society which he celebrates is doomed. We are entering the third world-historical period, the 'present age', in which order and hierarchy are being broken down by the levelling process. Kierkegaard's attitude to this is ambivalent: on the one hand, he sees levelling as destructive of much that is good, and even as threatening a new tyranny, far worse than that of any individual despot—the tyranny of the crowd. But, on the other hand, he sees that these social changes may make possible a new and richer form of individual responsibility, and, further away in the future, enable the development of a new form of genuine community, which, so far from suppressing individuality, is based on its fullest and richest development.

Kierkegaard's reaction to what I have called the ideal of disengagment is complex. He wholly opposes the drive towards a philosophy of the pure subject, and insists on the epistemological limits imposed on each 'existing spirit' by his finitude. But he constantly extols the individualism of the 'subjective thinker', who worries about his existential problems, and refuses simply to adopt the prevailing social and religious values. Social conformism is constantly under attack in Kierkegaard's writings, as we have seen above.

Given this attitude, we might expect Kierkegaard to support the overthrow of traditional social mores, and to encourage movements aimed at breaking down class distinctions, the uncritical respect for authority, and so on. For, by these means, individuals are forced to decide about ethical questions for themselves, rather than simply take their answers from social convention. Why, then, is Kierkegaard so hostile to political individualism and 'levelling'? I think there are two main reasons.

[19] *W of L* 58.   [20] Ibid.

First, he argues that to break down social conventions is to confuse the absolute, the religious, with the relative and temporal. As he argued in the passages from *Works of Love* that I quoted above, the spiritual equality of all people and the need for each of us to establish our individual relationship with God, does not mean that all political and social distinctions are broken down. These things are relativized and—ideally—transformed by a new ethical content, but they must remain. This is really part of Kierkegaard's resistance to abstraction, his insistence on the concrete realities of human life. Every one of us is born into a particular society in a particular historical period; this does not affect us essentially, for the essential task is the same for everyone—the God-relationship. But this does not mean that we can simply break with the world, with our wordly tasks and needs, and our position in society; we must combine an absolute concern for the absolute with a relative concern for the relative.

As little as the Christian lives or can live without a physical body, just as little can he live outside the differences of the earthly life to which every individual by birth, by condition, by circumstances, by education and so on, specially belongs—none of us is the pure man. Christianity is too earnest to talk nonsense about pure man, it only wishes to make all men pure.[21]

One can accept this religious point; we were not created as pure spirits, and therefore should not try to live as such, to the exclusion of our physical and social concerns. But this does not imply that we should rest content with the social institutions with which we happen to find ourselves. For that conclusion, Kierkegaard has to appeal either to a political argument to the effect that hierarchical structure and authority is necessary to any society, or to a religious doctrine that the Christian should concentrate on his eternal destiny, and not worry about such trivialities as social reform. Kierkegaard is sometimes drawn towards saying this,[22] though it stands in some contradiction to the view mentioned at the beginning of this paragraph. If one rejects, as I think one should, this radically other-wordly interpretation of Christianity, the argument for conservatism must rest on the purely political claim that all society must be hierarchical. This is a claim that Kierkegaard does endorse, but,

[21] Ibid.   [22] Cf. e.g. *Journals* 4151.

even one who accepts this point, may still argue that the existing hierarchy is unjust and needs to be radically changed.

Kierkegaard's second main objection to levelling is that it does not—directly, at least—lead to individualism at all, but tends to submerge the individual in the anonymous crowd; this, indeed, is the major theme in his social criticism. In previous societies each individual had a part to play in a particular community which was small enough for him to feel directly related to it. People accepted the differentiations in society which cut it into smaller subgroups, each with its own particular traditions and customs and sense of identity. The levelling tendency regards each individual not as a member of a particular nation or class or even sex, but only as a human being in the abstract—essentially no different from any other. However, this does not lead to genuine autonomy; the differences between people have all been flattened out, and, as a result, they all merge into the crowd, in which one individual is hardly distinguished from the rest. No longer regarding themselves as essentially related to anything else, people become 'reflective' about the relationships in which they do find themselves, eventually becoming incapable of spontaneity and passion. Instead of 'the loyal citizen who cheerfully does homage to his king, and now is embittered by his tyranny', we have one who thinks of himself as an 'outsider'. He 'does not relate himself in the relation, but is a spectator computing the problem: the relation of a subject to his king . . .'[23]

This passionless age Kierkegaard contrasts unfavourably with that of the French Revolution. Then people were related in enthusiasm to an ideal. 'When individuals (each one individually) are essentially and passionately related to an idea, and together are essentially related to the same idea, the relation is optimal and normative. Individually the relation separates them (each one has himself for himself), and ideally it unites them.'[24] Here we have a sketch of Kierkegaard's political ideal. In this passage he does not attempt to specify the content of the 'idea', being concerned, 'purely dialectically',[25] with the forms of society. He outlines two stages which are inferior to the ideal: 'If individuals relate to an idea merely en masse, (consequently without the individual separation of inwardness), we get violence, anarchy,

[23] *TA* 79.   [24] Ibid. 62.   [25] Ibid.

riotousness; but if there is no idea for the individuals en masse and no individually separating essential inwardness, either, then we have crudeness.'[26] The former stage was that of the Revolution, the latter is that of the 'Present Age'.

In this age people have no idea to which to relate; without actually abolishing existing social associations and relationships, they have undermined their significance by setting up the idea of 'pure humanity' as the only group to which a human being can be said to belong essentially. And—regarded just as human beings—we are all on the same level, and all distinctions are flattened out. 'No assemblage will be able to halt the abstraction of levelling . . . Not even national individuality will be able to halt it, for the abstraction of levelling is related to a higher negativity: pure humanity.'[27] This is the basis for Kierkegaard's polemic against the 'crowd', in which all individual excellence is submerged.

Kierkegaard's attitude to the levelling process is, however, ambivalent. Cutting the individual loose from his traditional social bonds may force him back into the anonymity of the crowd, but it may also force him to develop as an individual. 'Every individual, each one separately, may in turn be religiously educated, in the highest sense be helped to acquire the essentiality of the religious by means of the examen rigorosum of levelling.'[28] Regarding myself as a member of an 'organic' community, I may go along with its standards to the detriment of my individuality and—especially—of my relationship to God. But, with the breakdown of these communities and my spontaneous identification with, and loyalty to, them, I must either become a 'single individual' or sink into the abstract generality of the human race, 'pure humanity'. The situation is clarified, and there is far less temptation to lose myself in such a homogenous abstraction than in a particular, natural community.

For it is extremely comic to see the particular individual classed under the infinite abstraction 'pure humanity', without any middle term, since all the communal concretions of individuality that temper the comic by relativity and strengthen the relative pathos are annihilated. But this again expresses the fact that rescue comes only through the essentiality of the religious in the particular individual.[29]

[26] Ibid. 63.   [27] Ibid. 87.   [28] Ibid.   [29] Ibid. 88.

Precisely because communal life is disintegrating in the present age, the individual is thrown back on his own resources. If he is weak, he will seek refuge in the crowd, and simply go along with whatever—rapidly shifting—standards it adopts. ('A people, an assembly, a person, can change in such a way that one may say "they are no longer the same"; but the public can become the very opposite and is still the same—the public.'[30]) But if he has the strength for it, he can, stripped now of his social identity, work out his own salvation as a particular individual.

As a social critic, Kierkegaard noted the breakdown of the old forms of organic community, the rise of the disengaged ideal and, as a result, not only the autonomous individual, but also the anonymous crowd. In this new type of society people do not identify with any of the old 'communal concretions of individuality', or with the standards and norms that go with membership of such groups. But it is in that sort of organic society, composed of various smaller social organisms, that Judge William's type of ethics is at home. In the kind of society in which people identify themselves only as human beings, where they do not regard the fact that they are men or women, young or old, aristocrats or artisans as essentially defining them as persons and as prescribing fixed standards of behaviour, it can only seem anachronistic. When every individual classifies himself under the 'infinite abstraction "pure humanity", without any middle term', then we have the situation defended intellectually by liberal theorists; a basic 'social morality' regulates the activities of all people, and the main function of this is to prevent us treading on one another's toes as we each pursue our own 'individual ideals'.[31] And those who, within a liberal society, adhere to a more traditional conception of ethics, are usually understood by the liberals as simply pursuing some (from their standpoint, eccentric) ideal as individuals, which is not how they understand themselves.

In such a society the individual lacks clearly defined duties

[30] *TA* 92.

[31] The social morality may be defined in utilitarian terms or in terms of rights; the dispute between these conceptions is irrelevant here, as it is a dispute within liberalism. (Utilitarianism is not necessarily liberal in theory, but almost always is in practice.)

and rights deriving from his 'station'; the repentant aesthete has no stable network of institutions and norms into which to fit himself. There are only the virtues that can be justified as needful for anyone (as he classifies himself under the heading of pure humanity), and the personal commitments that he makes as an individual. And these are not so easily distinguished from the merely aesthetic commitments from which one can always 'sheer off at will' with each change of mood.

Within the contemporary disintegration of *Sittlichkeit*, the individual is, to some extent anyway, forced into disengagement. He may react to that by immersing himself in the crowd—that is, by adopting whatever values and norms the majority of people accept, following them as they change. This is different from the attitude of the ethicist, in that he adheres to a stable set of values defined by institutional roles; the crowd man goes along with public opinion, which is whatever 'the public' decides (or is influenced into deciding) it is at any moment. Or he may retain his individuality in personal commitments to freely chosen ground projects, which are without much institutional definition, and which must therefore generate their own norms and standards. It is accordingly difficult for this to avoid collapsing back into aestheticism. There remains Kierkegaard's preferred option: the leap of faith to the religious level, where each individual is related, as an individual, to a transcendental source of value.

It will no longer be as it once was, that individuals could look to the nearest eminence for orientation when things got somewhat hazy before their eyes. That time is now past. They either must be lost in the dizziness of abstract infinity or be saved essentially in the infinitude of the religious life . . . [T]he cruelty of abstraction exposes the vanity of the finite in itself; look—the abyss of the infinite is opening up; look— the sharp scythe of levelling permits all, every single one, to leap over the blade—look, God is waiting! Leap then, into the embrace of God.[32]

4.1.3. *To Will One Thing*

Judge William argued convincingly against aestheticism and for commitment to projects. But his belief that such commitment was to be found in the institutional roles of one's society both

[32] *TA* 108.

fails to do justice to individuality and is appearing increasingly to be an anachronism, inapplicable to modern society. The individual may still commit himself to projects. But what projects? Is this just a question that must be left to each individual to decide for himself, as in Sartrean existentialism? And how is the individual to order his projects? Which takes precedence when they conflict? Must this, too, be left up to the arbitrary will? Or to how the individual happens to feel at the time, which takes us back to aestheticism? This is the third problem—or set of problems—for a purely ethical standpoint; if there is no one overriding ground project, derived from the essence of human nature, there must be a constant threat of conflict within the moral life, between the demands of different projects to which the agent is committed, and these are rationally insoluble. Perhaps this is something that we will just have to learn to live with. Stuart Hampshire writes:

I have argued that human nature, conceived in terms of common human needs and capacities, always underdetermines a way of life, and underdetermines the moral prohibitions and injunctions that support a way of life. I am making three points against the classical moralists: a) that there cannot be such a thing as the complete human good; nor b) can there be a harmony amongst all the essential virtues in a complex life; nor c) can we infer what is universally the best way of life from propositions about human nature.[33]

If this is right, then the project of developing a neo-Aristotelian, naturalistic ethics collapses back into the subjectivism that it set out to oppose.

If the life of the virtues is continuously fractured by choices in which one allegiance entails the apparently arbitrary renunciation of another, it may seem that the goods internal to practices do after all derive their authority from our individual choices; for when different goods summon in different and incompatible directions, 'I' have to choose between their rival claims. The modern self with its criterionless choices apparently reappears in the alien context of what was claimed to be an Aristotelian world.[34]

[33] S. Hampshire, 'Morality and Conflict', in his *Morality and Conflict* (Oxford, 1983), 155.

[34] A. MacIntyre, *After Virtue: A Study in Moral Theory* (London, 1981), 188.

Philippa Foot, after arguing in the late 1950s against Hare's subjectivism, came in the early 1970s to see morality as a system of hypothetical imperatives, where it is up to the individual to decide whether or not he will volunteer to fight 'for liberty and justice'.[35]

Connected with this, is the problem of relativism. If one accepts that the projects to which one is committed, and the virtues which one cultivates, do not define *the* good way of life but only *a* good way, may this not weaken one's allegiance to them? Hampshire believes that, alongside a universal morality, prescribing certain standards that should be observed in treating everyone, there are also local moral systems to which we are—rightly—attached not because they are valid, according to any universal criteria, but because they are ours. 'Men and women . . . often do in fact implicitly distinguish between those duties which they think they cannot neglect simply as human beings, and those duties which they think arise from a valued way of life, which might, however regrettably, change radically . . .'[36] Hampshire wants to defend the latter sort of value against the utilitarian/Kantian demand that all values must be justified in universalistic terms. But is it really possible for us now to put behind us the centuries of Christianity, and the more recent tradition of the Enlightenment, and simply accept norms and customs because they are ours, without trying to find a further justification in universal moral standards? Can I accept that one action is right for me in a certain situation, and a quite different one for someone else? Can I commit myself with passion to a way of life, without believing it to be defensible in universal terms? Does not this sense that absolute foundations are missing for our social morality actually have the effect of undermining our commitment to it? Does not social morality need some absolute backing—a legitimization myth, if you like—to be convincing in itself, whether this backing is provided by God, by Reason (the Enlightenment), or by History (Hegel and Marx)? These are genuine, rather than merely rhetorical, questions, and no doubt none of them should be answered with a simple 'yes' or 'no'. But they are disturbing, none the less.

---

[35] P. Foot, 'Morality as a System of Hypothetical Imperatives', in her *Virtues and Vices, and Other Essays in Moral Philosophy* (Oxford, 1978).
[36] Hampshire, 'Morality and Conflict', 143.

These considerations are bringing us to a new either/or. Either we remain within the sphere of the ethical, accepting that it cannot provide justifications for universal benevolence or even justice, that it gives rise to rationally unresolvable conflicts between commitments which arise, in the last analysis, from arbitrary choice, that the clear institutional framework that separated the ethical decisively from the personal and aesthetic is crumbling; or we must opt for the religious. It is not the case that, 'if God is dead, then everything is permitted', but, without a religious backing, morality cannot have an absolute character, moral requirements cannot necessarily be considered over-riding,[37] one cannot discover a single best way of life, or any way of resolving moral dilemmas which is not in some way arbitrary. Ethics becomes pluralistic, conflict-ridden, rooted in personal decision. Someone who is searching for absolute values, for a firm foundation for his moral life, will not be satisfied. The rationale for making ethical commitments in the first place was that only in this way could selfhood be achieved, could the multiplicity in the individual's soul be resolved into a unity. But a non-religious ethics remains pluralistic. According to Kierkegaard, the factor that drives us from one stage of life to the next is an—at first unconscious and inchoate—desire for wholeness, for an ultimate integration and coherence in our lives. This is what brings us to make ethical commitments, but, if it is strong enough, it may drive us out of the ethical altogether in the search for an absolute *telos*, for the one thing to will, which can impose a unity on our lives.

An absolute *telos*, as I have argued above, cannot be derived from any purely naturalistic understanding of human nature. But in the religious sphere it is given; it is the primary, overriding task for each individual to bring him- or herself into the right relationship with God. This task takes absolute precedence over all other purposes and duties. If we can accept that there is an absolute *telos* of human life, then there is a clear and decisive answer to the basic existential question: How shall I live? My moral identity is made clear—what I am is given by my relation to the *telos*, and it is in action deriving from this relation that I become what I am. Whereas the Kantian asks, with regard to any action that he might be considering, whether it is

---

[37] Cf. P. Foot, 'Are Moral Considerations Overriding', in *Virtues and Vices*.

compatible with the conditions of rational agency, the religious man asks if it is compatible with the right development of his relationship to God.

There is a sharp contrast here, between the rational autonomy of Kantian ethics and the heteronomy of religious morality. Nevertheless, several commentators have attempted to interpret Kierkegaard along Kantian lines. And it is the edifying discourse *Purity of Heart is to Will One Thing*, Kierkegaard's fullest exploration of commitment to an absolute *telos*, which has been the chief victim of these misunderstandings—by, for instance, Hannay and by Jeremy Walker.[38] They see very close parallels between Kierkegaard's notion of willing one thing, and Kant's insistence that one should only will those maxims which are capable of being universally willed. I have already said that I do not think Kierkegaard's moral philosophy is at all Kantian, and to interpret it in this way is a radical error. Kierkegaard's whole concern is with self-realization, the individual's quest for fulfilment. It is this that drives Kierkegaardian man to accept the universal disciplines of ethics and religion, not any Kantian concern for consistency in action. Kierkegaard certainly had some respect for Kant, and was, I think, somewhat influenced by his epistemology; but, given Kierkegaard's existential pre-occupations, I cannot see how he could have regarded Kant's very abstract ethics of the pure rational agent as anything more than the sort of rubbish that a 'professor' would talk about ethics. In one of his very few references to Kant's moral philosophy, in the *Journals*, he dismisses the fundamental idea of self-legislation with contempt.

Kant held that man was his own law (autonomy), i.e. bound himself under the law he gave himself. In a deeper sense, that means to say: lawlessness or experimentation. It is no harder than the thwacks which Sancho Panza applied to his own bottom. I can no more be really stricter in A than I am or than I wish myself to be, in B. There must be some compulsion, if it is to be a serious matter. If I am not bound by anything higher than myself, and if I am to bind myself, where am I to acquire the severity as A by which as B, I am to be bound, so long as A and B are the same?[39]

---

[38] Cf. Hannay, *Kierkegaard*, ch. 6, and J. Walker, *To Will One Thing: Reflections on Kierkegaard's 'Purity of Heart'* (Montreal and London, 1972), passim.

[39] Dru 1041.

To be sure, in Kierkegaard the individual chooses himself, but he does this in choosing to submit himself to the external discipline of social institutions in the first place, and, in the second, to God.

The Kantian misinterpretation of Kierkegaard is not just a grotesque error, though. There are real parallels between the two thinkers. But this is because Kant's starting-point—the 'common rational knowledge of morality', for which he tried to find foundations within the structure of practical reason—was the set of ethical beliefs of a Christian society, more specifically a Lutheran one, strongly influenced by Pietism. From the Torah, via Christianity, Kant takes over the conception of morality as a set of laws which are absolute and overriding; he adopts also the Augustinian stress on the good will. The trouble is that he takes these historically specific ideas as being constitutive of the essence of morality as such, and then tries—and fails—to show that they are generated by the conditions of rational agency. (This diagnosis of what Kant was doing can be found in Schopenhauer;[40] it has been restated in our time by Anscombe.[41]) Therefore, it is no surprise that Kant often sounds like a Christian moralist such as Kierkegaard. But Kant's version of Christian ethics leaves out its presupposition and the condition of its intelligibility—namely, belief in God. (God does come in later, of course; but, for Kant, morality is a presupposition of religion, not vice versa.)

Walker, in advancing his Kantian interpretation of *Purity of Heart*, has to adopt a quite different reading of Kierkegaard's whole *œuvre* from the one I have outlined so far. I do not find this at all plausible, though I do not have the space to criticize it here. But I should mention his claim that in *Purity of Heart* Kierkegaard 'deliberately give[s] to his discussion an ethical import, as contrasted with a Christian one . . . the bulk of the book is cast quite unmistakably in terms specific to an ethics that is not Christian. For instance, God is referred to throughout by means of the Platonising term "the Good".'[42] This is to miss Kierkegaard's point that between the ethical and Christianity

[40] A. Schopenhauer, *On the Basis of Morality*, trans. E. F. J. Payne (Indianapolis, 1965), ch. 2.
[41] Cf. G. E. M. Anscombe, 'Modern Moral Philosophy', *Philosophy*, 1958.
[42] Walker, *To Will One Thing*, 5.

proper lies a general religiousness which is not specifically Christian. *Purity of Heart* is written at the level of this 'Religiousness A', but it is still a work of religious ethics, in which the good will is identified in thoroughly heteronomous fashion by reference to the object that it wills. Kierkegaard, in fact, uses a variety of locutions here—'God', 'the good', 'eternity', 'the eternal'; this vagueness is appropriate to the theologically unspecific level of Religiousness A. This does not alter the fact that, for Kierkegaard, the will can only become single, and thus 'pure', if it is directed to a higher power wholly other than what it is. *Purity of Heart* is, therefore, radically anti-Kantian.

Kierkegaard is concerned to show how 'double-mindedness' is overcome in religious commitment, and that it cannot be overcome in any other way. But what does he mean by 'double-mindedness'? It is the condition of someone who has no one, overriding, unconditional purpose. He has various different aims and goals in life, no one of which takes precedence over the others. He wills what he wills to a certain extent, but not unconditionally; or he wills something not for its own sake, but for the sake of something else. (The last category is important for Kierkegaard's attack on hypocrisy—willing the good out of expectation of reward or punishment—but this is not something that I will be discussing further here.) He who is double-minded has no one, central, guiding thread running through his life, no one unifying aim to give coherence to his life plan. As we saw, this is the condition of the aesthete, but it is that of the ethicist also. He wills to be a good husband, a good father, a good judge, a good citizen, a good friend . . . ; but what happens when what is required of him in one of these roles conflicts with what is required of him in another? Such dramatic conflicts may be rare occurrences in a person's life, but, when they do occur, they may serve to show up its existing fragmentation. I have argued that a person needs to find the unity of a narrative in his or her life, but the ethicist, pursuing his various obligations, filling his various social roles, may find that there is no overall narrative pattern in his life. There are several different narratives—of his working life, of his family life, of his friendships and leisure activities—but they develop in parallel, without any very close connection between them. Like the aesthete, he, too, finds his life disintegrating into a collection of fragments, even if they are larger fragments than the aesthete's. Even if one thinks less in terms of social roles than of personal ground projects, which need not be socially defined, the problem still arises of possible collisions between these projects which reveal the self to be fragmented into a collection of different role-players.

One may choose to put up with this situation, if that is what our situation is. Or even learn to celebrate it, as Rawls does. 'Human good is heterogeneous, because the self is heterogeneous. Although to subordinate all our aims to one end does not strictly speaking violate the principle of rational choice . . . it still strikes us as irrational, or more likely as mad. The self is disfigured and put in the service of one of its ends for the sake of system.'[43] Alternatively, one might, by one's own free choice, decide to give one's life the strong kind of unity which Kierkegaard demands. One might choose single-mindedly to devote oneself to politics, to art or science, to one's career or children or marriage, to charity and works of altruism, or to some more esoteric ideal. Kierkegaard discusses this 'devilish wisdom' that would find salvation in single-minded willing, irrespective of what it is that is willed. He introduces a proto-Nietzschean figure, who proclaims: 'Unless it wills one thing, a man's life is sure to become one of wretched mediocrity, of pitiful misery. He must will one thing, regardless of whether it be good or bad. He must will one thing, for therein lies a man's greatness.'[44]

In reply to this, Kierkegaard claims that such an individual remains double-minded. First, try as he might, he cannot escape a longing for 'the good', for something to which he can commit himself absolutely because it is absolutely worthy of this commitment. As it is, our proto-Superman has nothing to which to give himself except his own will. He has chosen to make some goal his absolute *telos* not because of any inherent value that it may have, but just because he must will something absolutely, and, ultimately, it becomes irrelevant exactly what it is that he

---

[43] J. Rawls, *A Theory of Justice* (Oxford, 1986), 554. Of course, what Kierkegaard—like Aristotle and Aquinas, to whom Rawls explicitly refers in this section—has in mind is not any such Procrustean operation, but the integration of the personality, with all its complexity. The variety of goods is not denied; what is provided is a criterion for their ordering.   [44] *P of H* 55.

wills. This brings us to the second sense in which he can be called double-minded. The strong-willed character claims to will only one thing; yet the actual object is, in a deeper sense, without importance to him. He really just wills to will. But to will without willing anything in particular is impossible; so he ends up willing absolutely something to which he is ultimately indifferent. Thirdly, Kierkegaard argues that only the 'eternal' can be willed absolutely. For nothing temporal is, in fact, a unity; on closer examination, it turns out to be complex, and, in willing it, one does not will one thing but several. 'For pleasure and honour and riches and power and all that this world has to offer only appear to be one thing.' One cannot 'be said to will one thing when that one thing which he wills is not in itself one'.[45]

Furthermore, and fourthly, though there are many goods in the world, none is absolutely good, worthy of absolute commitment. To make some temporal good one's whole aim and purpose in life is soul-destroying. Consider someone who commits himself absolutely even to something that is, in itself, a serious object of ethical striving. The fanatic who sacrifices everything to his political cause; the businessman who lives only for his work; even someone who only lives for some hobby or sport: these are all pathetic, and often dangerous, figures. The parent who 'lives for' his or her children is liable to be a suffocating menace to them. Two lovers who live only for each other lock themselves into an egoism *à deux*, and are liable to destroy each other by demanding more from a human relationship than any human being can possibly give. If the only goods in existence are temporal ones, then Rawls is right. If there can be an absolute *telos*, something that can be willed absolutely and single-mindedly, then it cannot be anything in this world. Either we abandon the search for an absolute *telos*, and with it the notion of absolute ethical standards—and so abandon the search for the kind of unified selfhood with which Kierkegaard is concerned—or we make the leap of faith. But, of course, in the Kierkegaardian world—and I believe that it is our world—there are no guarantees. The desire for the absolute, the 'infinite longing' of which Kierkegaard speaks so eloquently, may be

[45] Ibid. 49–50.

delusive; the leap into the religious may be a leap into thin air. We must either give up the infinite longing or transcend the merely ethical; but there is nothing that can tell us which is the right choice to make.

If, then, we are to achieve that ultimate coherence and integration of our lives, the desire for which Kierkegaard posits as the force driving us on through the spheres of existence, we must turn from spiritual self-sufficiency in order to relate ourselves to God. Only in this relation can the disharmony in our existence finally be resolved. In *The Sickness unto Death* Kierkegaard schematically reviews the options. Outside religion we can either in despair not will to be ourselves (submerging ourselves in mindless conformity, or dissipating ourselves in aestheticism), or in despair will to be ourselves (in the self-sufficiency of the ethical, or in Nietzschean self-assertion). In none of these ways can we avoid despair or find self-integration. Only by turning our backs on the dream of human autonomy and self-sufficiency—whether in its hedonistic or its moralistic form, whether Kantian or Nietzschean—can we find fulfilment. 'The formula that describes the state of the self when despair is completely rooted out is this: in relating itself to itself and in willing to be itself, the self rests transparently in the power that established it.'[46]

It remains to be seen what this resting in God means in practice. How does religious commitment change an individual's life? What does it involve him in doing? And, granted that it involves a leap beyond the ethical, should it be thought of as supplementing it or as contradicting it? The concluding section will follow Kierkegaard's discussion of these questions.

4.2. THE RELIGIOUS

Granted that religious commitment brings a new factor into the moral life, how radical is the change that it brings about there? I do not intend to provide a detailed commentary on, or an evaluation of, Kierkegaard's religious writings—that would require another book and, perhaps, another kind of book. In

[46] *SUD* 14.

this section I will be concerned with two main themes. First, given that religion involves commitment to an absolute *telos*, what does this mean in practice? What is the relation between the absolute good and the various relative goods? These questions are, it is worth noting, relevant even to a non-religious ethics, if it has a concept of the absolute good (although I have expressed my doubts already about the viability of such an ethics). Secondly, I want to consider the possibility of a religious outlook that is suggested in some of Kierkegaard's writings, which would represent not a development of teleological thinking about ethics but a radical break with it.

A good place to begin the reconstruction of Kierkegaard's argument is with Judge William. He is, by his own lights, a religious man. References to God, repentance, sin, and faith occur quite frequently in his letters. And he sees no disharmony between the ethical and the religious. But this is because, in the last resort, his religion is a sort of metaphysical epiphenomenon of his ethics—a halo on its head, but no part of its body. In providing my reconstruction of the ethical stage, I did not feel the need to introduce any religious concepts, and I do not think that this omission does anything to distort the fundamental argument of Judge William. Even when he uses religious phrases, it often turns out that what he means by them is not essentially religious at all. I have already quoted James Collins's remark that, for the Judge, repentance turns out to be 'more an honest recognition of the individual in his concrete nature, than a religious sorrow over sinfulness'.[47] In a couple of places Kierkegaard makes the Judge say things which have echoes in the Gospels, but at places where very different things are said. According to Judge William, 'man is born only once, and there is no probability of a repetition.'[48] But in John's Gospel we read: 'Except a man be born again, he cannot see the kingdom of God.'[49] Later Judge William quotes approvingly from Ecclesiasticus (from 'Jesus the son of Sirach'): 'who shall trust a man that hath no nest and lodgeth wheresoever he findeth himself at nightfall?',[50] but a later Jesus tells us: 'The foxes have holes, and the birds of the air *have* nests; but the Son of man hath not where

[47] J. Collins, *The Mind of Kierkegaard* (Princeton, NJ, 1983), 84–5.
[48] *E/O* ii. 41.   [49] John 3: 3.   [50] *E/O* ii. 82.

to lay *his* head.'[51] A few pages later, Judge William chides 'A' for liking to describe himself as 'a stranger and a pilgrim in the world'. The Judge agrees that 'this phrase might well be used of you',[52] and clearly thinks that it is not good that this should be so. But, however much mockery or cynicism there may be in 'A' 's appropriation of the phrase, there is a core of sincerity, and it is at this point that the disillusioned, detached aesthete may be closer to the religious than the solid bourgeois is.

This is not to suggest that there is anything in the least insincere about the Judge's religious professions; nevertheless, he has failed really to understand the religion that he professes. For him, being a Christian is like being husband or a judge—it is one of the roles that one adopts as a good member of society. He has no conception of religion as a possible threat to the established social order. (He does consider a type of ascetic mysticism that might be; but he considers it to be a more primitive form of religion, long since superseded by a respectable Christianity.) His outlook is essentially secular, and his religion is an adjunct to his ethics. His position is that of one who accepts a certain religion because it is bound up with the culture, history, and traditions of the society with which he identifies. This is one way of reducing religion to ethics; the Kantian vision of absolute moral laws and the autonomy of the ethical is another. Neither is compatible with Christianity as it understands itself.

The diffrence between Christian morality and the Judge's social ethics is first brought out in the concluding item in *Either/ Or*—a sermon on 'The Edification Implied in the Thought that, as against God, we Are always in the Wrong'. Now Judge William gives no sign of thinking that he is always in the wrong; on the contrary, he insists that one can succeed ethically. By willing to become a self, I can become a self—by ethical striving, I can resolve the disharmonies of existence into a coherent unity. The Judge is happy in his marriage, in his work; he is confident that he has solved 'the great riddle of living in eternity and yet hearing the hall clock strike'.[53] Yet, according to Christianity, he, like everyone else, is in the wrong before God. If this is so, ethical commitment and good citizenship alone are

[51] Matthew, 8: 20.   [52] *E/O* ii. 85.   [53] Ibid. 141.

not enough to solve the problem of existence. The Judge's purely ethical religion is not Christianity, and one should not muddy the waters by pretending that it is. Even religiousness A goes far beyond the ethical, though it is doubtful whether this distinction between Christianity and 'natural religion' was clear in Kierkegaard's mind when he wrote *Either/Or*. But in the *Postscript* we are told that 'The edifying element in the sphere of religiousness A is essentially that of immanence, it is the annihilation by which the individual puts himself out of the way in order to find God.'[54] This sounds like the mystical asceticism that Judge William explicitly condemns in *Either/Or* (ii. 245–55) and in *Stages on Life's Way*, where he remarks that one who forgoes marriage on religious grounds 'crosses out the whole of earthly life in one single stroke, and retains only eternity and spiritual interests which admittedly at first glance are not slight, but in the *longitude of time* are very strenuous and also in one way or another an expression for an unhappy life'.[55] But Johannes Climacus dismisses the Judge's more affirmative view of religion: 'the most exuberant sense of well-being in the delight of immanence . . . is a very lovable thing, but not edifying, and not essentially a God-relationship.'[56]

Religion, then, is more radically disturbing than the Judge is prepared to admit. In the remainder of this section I will try to show just how radical that disturbance is. First (4.2.1), I will examine Kierkegaard's notorious argument in *Fear and Trembling*, that religion can require a 'teleological suspension of the ethical'. Secondly (4.2.2), I will examine the account of religion given in the *Philosophical Fragments* and the *Postscript*, with its distinction between Religiousness A and Religiousness B. Finally (4.2.3), I will discuss some of the themes of Kierkegaard's later, more directly religious writings.

4.2.1. *The Teleological Suspension of the Ethical*

Kierkegaard's best known discussion of the relationship between ethics and religious faith is found in *Fear and Trembling*. Abraham's willingness to sacrifice his son makes him a hero of faith, although, on ethical grounds, he must be regarded simply

---

[54] *CUP* 497.   [55] *SLW* 101.   [56] *CUP* 497.

as a murderer. The main point of the book is to demonstrate that religion transcends ethics; not only does the religious believer have specifically religious reasons to do things that ethics does not enjoin, but he may even have religious reason to do things that ethics can only condemn. At the same time, Kierkegaard makes a distinction between two kinds of religion. One is represented by the figure of the 'knight of infinite resignation', the other by the 'knight of faith'. Both are distinguished from a third paradigmatic character, the 'tragic hero', who remains within the confines of the ethical. Kierkegaard's pseudonym, Johannes *de silentio*, can understand and admire the tragic hero and the knight of infinite resignation; but Abraham, the knight of faith, he can only admire; he cannot understand him. But this makes him all the more vehement in rejecting those who would try to understand Abraham by reducing his faith to some lower and more easily comprehended category.

Johannes presents three *problemata*: (i) Is there a teleological suspension of the ethical? (ii) Is there an absolute duty to God? and (iii) Was it ethically defensible for Abraham to conceal his undertaking? The discussion of the third problem is actually the longest and the richest in aesthetic detail, but the main philosophical issues are brought out most clearly in the first two. Accordingly, I shall concentrate on them. Johannes does not come to any explicit conclusions; his work, one might say, is one of conceptual clarification, which leaves the reader to make up his own mind. In each *problema* he begins by giving a characterization of the ethical, regarded as the highest stage of human life. This may be right, says Johannes, but, if it is, if Hegel is justified in regarding individual self-assertion 'as a "moral form of evil" . . . which must be annulled',[57] if he is right that there 'is nothing incommensurable in a human life',[58] then he is in flagrant self-contradiction when he admires and praises Abraham as the father of faith, for he has already 'pronounced judgement both on Abraham and on faith'.[59] From a consistently ethical point of view, Abraham 'ought to be sent back to a lower court and shown up as a murderer'.[60] If faith was what led him to prepare to kill Isaac, then faith is incommensurable with the ethical, and the consistent ethicist will not regard 'father of faith'

---

[57] *FT* 54.   [58] Ibid. 68.
[59] Ibid. 68–9.   [60] Ibid. 55.

as a praiseworthy title at all. Faith must be combated in the name of ethics.

What conception of ethics is Kierkegaard working with here? He seems to be thinking in terms of social morality, *Sittlichkeit*, as the references to Hegel suggest. James Bogen writes: 'Kierkegaard speaks as though morality were a system of duties.'[61] He elaborates on what he means by this. 'In everyday life, we usually speak of the duties of parents, children, friends, citizens, employees and members of clubs and organisations, while we do not speak of the duties of human beings qua human beings . . . we are said to acquire duties, not . . . simply by being born into the species *Homo sapiens* . . but by occupying definite positions in society.'[62] I agree that Kierkegaard seems to use this conception of morality as a system of such 'positional duties' in *Fear and Trembling*. And, as I have argued, that is the conception of morality that emerges from, and receives its (partial) justification in, the letters of Judge William. Donnelly criticizes Bogen on this point, arguing that there are more Kantian and universalist overtones in Johannes *de silentio*'s conception of the ethical.[63] This may be so, but Bogen is right when he says that the ethical in *Fear and Trembling* is primarily the sphere of positional duties. As he notes, the examples of tragic heroism presuppose such an understanding of ethics. Obviously, though, Abraham is as much a scandal to Kantian *Moralität* as to Hegelian *Sittlichkeit*. Kant writes: 'even though something is represented as commanded by God . . . yet, if it flatly contradicts morality, it cannot, despite all appearances be of God (for example, were a father ordered to kill his son, who is, so far as he knows, perfectly innocent).[64] Kant is at least consistent; it seems that he would have no hesitation in sending Abraham back to the lower court. Clearly, someone who believes in a universal and absolute moral law which holds good irrespective of the existence of God will not believe that religion can legitimately introduce radically new modes of behaviour;

---

[61] J. Bogen, 'Kierkegaard and the Teleological Suspension of the Ethical', *Inquiry* (1962), 306.   [62] Ibid. 308.

[63] Cf. J. Donnelly, 'Kierkegaard's Problem I and Problem II: An Analytic Perspective', in R. L. Perkins (ed.), *Kierkegaard's 'Fear and Trembling': Critical Appraisals* (Montgomery, Ala., 1981).

[64] I. Kant, *Religion Within the Limits of Reason Alone*, trans. T. M. Greene and H. H. Hudson (New York, 1960), 81–2.

nor will someone who thinks of religion as a sanctification of the prevailing social norms. Kierkegaard is concerned to show that, to be consistent, both must repudiate Christianity, since that does demand a transcendence of the purely ethical.

If we think of morality as a system of positional duties, the problem of a clash of duties may arise. As a parent, Agamemnon has one duty; as a king, he has a conflicting one. This is the agony of the tragic hero. Johannes *de silentio* seems to have no doubt about which duty must take precedence. Familial, paternal duty must be sacrificed—along with the child—in favour of duty to the state. We would hardly think this self-evident. Nor, as far as one could tell, would Judge William, who writes: 'marriage I regard them as the highest *telos* of individual life'[65]—in which case, it presumably takes precedence over the *telos* of citizenship or even kingship. This is one of the weaknesses of the purely ethical, that it gives us no idea of how to solve such conflicts. For Johannes, the agony of the tragic hero is that he must abandon one duty for the sake of his loyalty to a higher duty. Agamemnon may wish that he were not the king; but the king remains what he is, and, to act as king, he must teleologically suspend his ethical duty towards his daughter. 'The father will turn away his face, but the hero must raise the knife.'[66]

Though he was not unaware of the problem of indeterminacy in ordering one's duties (in other words, placing in order of relative importance the positions one holds, the projects to which one is committed), Kierkegaard puts this problem on one side. So, his examples of tragic heroes assume that we are dealing with people who were ethically justified in committing what would appear to be, on the face of it, distinctly unethical acts. The justification consists in appealing to a higher *telos*, a higher set of duties which override the first set. But the tragic hero remains within the sphere of the ethical. 'Abraham's situation is different. By his act he transgressed the ethical altogether, and had a higher *telos* outside it, in relation to which he suspended it.'[67] The point is that Abraham acted as an individual. What he did had no relation to the universal; none of his roles—as father, husband, head of a household, leader of a

<hr>

[65] *SLW* 101.   [66] *FT* 57.   [67] Ibid. 59.

tribe—demanded that he should kill Isaac. If they had, his act could be understood: anyone in the same position would have faced the same demand. But the call to sacrifice Isaac comes from Abraham's personal, individual relation to God. He does not act in fulfilment of the duties imposed by any social role. He does not act so as to benefit the nation or to maintain the laws, to which he has a higher duty than to his own family. He does not act on behalf of any putative universal 'moral law'. 'Why then, does Abraham do it? For God's sake and—the two are wholly identical—for his own sake.'[68] If Abraham is justified in his action, he is justified as the single individual in defiance of the universal ethical norms, all of which insist that the killing of Isaac would be a great evil. 'The story of Abraham contains, then, a teleological supension of the ethical. As the single individual he becomes higher than the universal. This is the paradox which cannot be mediated.'[69]

Problema 2 asks if there is an absolute duty to God. A certain ethical piety proclaims that all duties are duties to God, but this means that no duty in particular is a duty to God, and He is politely pushed away over the horizon. 'The whole existence of the human race rounds itself off as a perfect self-contained sphere . . . God comes to be an invisible vanishing point, an impotent thought; his power is only in the ethical, which fills all of existence.'[70] However, a different perspective is provided by the biblical injunction 'Thou shalt love the Lord thy God with all thy heart, and with all thy soul, and with all thy mind. This is the first and great commandment.'[71] As Kierkegaard points out, 'If this duty is absolute, then the ethical is reduced to the relative.'[72] Only if this is so, if there is an absolute duty to God, can Abraham's conduct be justified. For 'The ethical expression for his relation to Isaac is that the father must love the son. This ethical relation is reduced to the relative in contradistinction to the absolute relation to God.'[73] None of this should imply that the ethical is abrogated. That our absolute duty to God relativizes our duties to our fellow men does not mean that we should become cool or indifferent to those we love; it means that, however intensely we love them, the duty to God comes

---

[68] Ibid. [69] Ibid. 66. [70] Ibid. 68.
[71] Matthew 22: 37–8. [72] FT 70. [73] Ibid. 70–1.

first. It is because human duties and commitments are so important and so deeply felt that the knight of faith must feel such anguish in being called upon to suspend them. Nor can he even know—he can never prove—that he is being so called. 'Whether the single individual actually is undergoing a spiritual trial or is a knight of faith, only the single individual himself can decide.'[74] To journey out beyond ethics is to find oneself alone—perhaps with God, perhaps just alone.

What emerges from *Fear and Trembling* is that, if religion is regarded as the relationship of each individual to his absolute *telos*, it involves a relativization of all duties deriving from other relationships, and may call for their suspension. Hence, Kierkegaard rejects the Judge William-like view that would include the religious within the ethical. This does not, however, imply that the ethical and the religious are wholly distinct and discontinuous. Kierkegaard's own position in *Fear and Trembling* is, in fact, left ambiguous; this ambiguity is brought to light in a dispute between two of his commentators. Bogen argues that Kierkegaard has shown there to be a teleological suspension of the ethical, but—precisely because this is the case—holds that there is no absolute duty to God.[75] Donnelly, criticizing Bogen, argues the reverse; there is an absolute duty, and therefore no teleological suspension.

Bogen's argument is that, because religion suspends the ethical, it is wrong to use an ethical term like 'duty' to describe our relation to God. He has in mind, of course, his own characterization of ethics as the sphere of 'positional' duties, which emerge from social roles and make definite and predictable demands on us. We do not have a duty to God in this sense—what the believer does have is a willingness to obey God's commands, whatever they may be. As an occupant of social roles, I know what sort of demands will be made on me, what sort of things I will be expected to do; as an individual believer, I have no idea what God demands until He tells me. Donnelly, by contrast, wants to assimilate the position of the believer to that of the ethical person. As an agent in social life, I have various duties, some of which take precedence over others. Beyond

[74] FT 79.
[75] Bogen, 'Kierkegaard and the Teleological Suspension of the Ethical', 314–15.

them is my position in relationship to God. This is not exactly a social role, but here, too, I have obligations that arise out of a relationship. What these obligations may be is not predictable in detail in advance, but then neither are the obligations that may arise from such social roles as friendship or marriage. Nor does the relationship to God consist simply of a readiness to do anything at all when I hear a voice from the sky telling me to do it. The great religions claim that God has revealed His will in general terms—either laying down detailed laws, as in the Koran or the Torah, or at least general standards of behaviour and maxims.

For Donnelly, then, there is no teleological suspension of the ethical. Because I have an absolute duty to God, I can relativize or suspend other duties in relation to this—higher—duty. But, in so doing, I am following the normal pattern of ethical reasoning. Abraham's case is not essentially different from those of the tragic heroes Agamemnon, Jephthah, or Brutus. In all these cases, there is a duty to the child—but also a higher duty which overrides it. Abraham's duty is higher again; it would justify his suspending his duty to the state, were that called for—but we are not taken into a wholly new and different sphere.

Donnelly's position seems to be close to the mainstream of Christian—certainly of Catholic—ethical thought, which has generally taken over the structure of secular ethics, rather than attempting to transform it radically. Aquinas adopts Aristotle's ethics, agreeing that he had identified various earthly goods and the virtues which allow us to attain them. However, informed by revelation—which was, of course, unavailable to Aristotle— Aquinas claims that the final goal, the ultimate good for man, is not natural but supernatural—the eternal 'beatific vision' of God. And, to reach that good, we need other virtues that Aristotle did not discuss—faith, hope, and love (and, indeed, humility, of which he disapproved). In this way, it seems that religion, rather than threatening ethics, rounds it out and completes it. This is all the more true if we are less confident—as we should be—than Aristotle was of discovering the final good for man in naturalistic terms. Looking at the matter empirically, there seem to be various goods, various goals, but no one goal that can be considered to provide the ultimate aim of human striving. But, as I have argued, a teleological, neo-Aristotelian ethic without a conception of an ultimate good is a somewhat ramshackle structure. A religious ethic, providing a conception of one overriding good, seems to allow us to overcome these difficulties.

To a large extent, Kierkegaard does accept this general outlook. For him, selfhood is realized by making commitments and by developing the relevant virtues. These commitments are made first to social relationships, but then, impelled by our need for an absolute *telos*, to God. The basic structure of thought here remains teleological, Aristotelian. I am seeking a definite good— that is, to develop my relationships, first to other people, then to God. In order to obtain this good, I seek to develop the virtues necessary to these relationships, and to undertake the duties arising from them. Kierkegaard does not resolve the difficulty in *Fear and Trembling* to which I have drawn attention—that if the God-relationship is simply regarded as the highest of the various goals towards which I am striving, then the relativization of other goals does not constitute a radial break with ethical thinking. His main point, in any case, is to show that the religious cannot be reduced to a social ethics; whether or not religious demands are themselves thought of as ethical, religion may involve a suspension of whatever was regarded as ethical on a non-religious view. However, elsewhere in *Fear and Trembling* there is a distinction drawn between two types of religious outlook, one of which seems to involve a much more radical break with the structures of teleological ethics.

Abraham's willingness to sacrifice Isaac at God's command is taken by Kierkegaard as a symbol of the religious believer's willingness to renounce, if necessary, all worldly goods for the sake of his relationship to God. Because this is the ultimate good, no relative goods must be allowed to interfere with it. For the sake of my relation to the absolute, I may have to make the movement of what Kierkegaard calls 'infinite resignation', and renounce all other goods. But this attitude *per se* is not faith. In faith I not only renounce all finite, temporal goods—I also receive them back again. According to the Kantian and Hegelian views that Kierkegaard is combating, I perform my duty to God simply by performing my worldly duties; I realize the good of a relationship to God simply by enjoying a proper relationship to wordly goods. According to the attitude of infinite resignation, the relationship to God is something quite distinct from all other goods, and must be pursued if not by rejecting them, at least by radically relativizing them. But in the attitude of faith, after having made the infinite resignation, I receive back all that I offered up. Instead of abandoning the finite to struggle painfully towards the infinite, I live with contentment and joy in the finite—precisely by virtue of my relationship to the infinite. This seems to suggest an outlook in which the relationship to God is not one good among others—even if the highest, for which the others have to be renounced. It becomes incommensurable with other goods.

The act of resignation does not require faith, for what I gain in resignation is my eternal consciousness. This is a purely philosophical movement . . . It takes a purely human courage to renounce the whole temporal realm in order to gain eternity . . . But it takes a paradoxical and humble courage to grasp the whole temporal realm now by virtue of the absurd, and this is the courage of faith.[76]

Of course, to renounce the temporal for the eternal requires faith, in the sense that one needs to have faith in the reality of 'the eternal', in the existence of God. But Kierkegaard is using 'faith' here to mean something more than this. Infinite resignation remains purely human, purely philosophical, because it still follows the standard pattern of ethical thought. It identifies the absolute *telos*; and, by so doing, shows that it is reasonable for me to renounce all other goods, if necessary, so as to attain this one. Faith, on the other hand, is absurd. It makes the same renuciation; but then believes that what has been renounced will be returned. Abraham is willing to sacrifice Isaac, but has faith that, ultimately, this will not be required of him. This is not based on any calculation of probability or likeliness, but on 'the absurd', on faith in the grace of God. There is no point in explaining to a knight of faith that this is unreasonable—he knows that already. 'Consequently, he can be saved only by the absurd and this he grasps by faith.'[77]

Philosophical reasoning can understand that certain goods should be renounced for the sake of a higher good. Much of religion has precisely this theme—that we should leave behind

[76] FT 48–9.　　　[77] Ibid. 47.

the lower, wordly goods in order to strive for the true good: the infinite, the eternal. The structure is teleological—the aim of life is to strive towards an absolute good, and relative goods may have to be abandoned *en route*. But in *Fear and Trembling* faith seems to be something quite different. It is not just something that is called up in rare moments of desperate crisis. Like infinite resignation, it is an attitude to the whole of life which is dramatically revealed by crises such as Abraham's. But whereas infinite resignation represents a process of dying away to the finite, the temporal, faith means 'To exist in such a way that my contrast to existence constantly expresses itself as the most beautiful and secure harmony with it'.[78]

Kierkegaard illustrates this with his imaginative portrayal of such a knight of faith. His 'infinitely resigned' pseudonym Johannes *de silentio* expresses astonishment:

'Good Lord, is this the man . . . he looks just like a tax collector!' But this is indeed the one. I move a little closer to him, watch his slightest movement to see if it reveals a bit of heterogeneous optical telegraphy from the infinite, a glance, a facial expression, a gesture, a sadness, a smile, that would betray the infinite in its heterogeneity with the finite. No! . . . he belongs entirely to the world; no bourgeois philistine could belong to it more.[79]

Unlike the 'religious' man, internally divided and suffering as he struggles to realize his eternal *telos*, the knight of faith is able to live in the finite, contentedly and without anxiety, precisely because he knows himself to be rooted in the eternal:

he has felt the pain of renouncing everything, the most precious thing in the world, and yet the finite tastes just as good to him as to one who never knew anything higher . . . he has this security that makes him delight in it as if finitude were the surest thing of all. And yet, yet, the whole earthly figure he presents is a new creation by virtue of the absurd. He resigned everything infinitely and then he grasped everything again by virtue of the absurd.[80]

In this account of faith I think Kierkegaard is ultimately relying on the Lutheran doctrine of salvation by grace. Man is so depraved, so far fallen, that he is unable to realize his *telos* by his own efforts, no matter how strenuously he struggles. But if he understands this, he may realize that there is no need to

---

[78] FT 50.   [79] Ibid. 39.   [80] Ibid. 40.

struggle. From his side he is quite unable to relate to God; but the relationship is nevertheless upheld and maintained from the other side, by God. Ethics then ceases to be a striving to realize a *telos*, but becomes simply an outlook of trust and gratitude. Bernard Williams, in fact, uses this doctrine as a counter-example to the thesis that ethics is necessarily concerned with human happiness and with the striving to reach a goal, though the version that he discusses is one which has no certainty about grace.

The point is that there is no means open to man towards reconciliation with God, no set of human projects conceivably adequate to secure this result—the gap is too great, and there is merely one sign of hope, Jesus Christ, that God's grace will lift up the undeserving. The devout man will obey the will of God as best he can in his forlorn condition, but not in order to secure for himself or anyone else, salvation, which is at best a wild hope; and if he is rejected, he can have no complaint.[81]

This does seem to me to be a radically different outlook from that of the ethical as I have discussed it so far. It represents a radical abandonment of human autonomy, of the notion that we are able to—or should—find the completion or fulfilment of our lives by our own efforts. Though this was Kierkegaard's view, his emphasis usually lies elsewhere; he felt that the Protestantism of his day had taken the doctrine of grace as a means of absolving itself from the need to make strenuous moral or religious effort. After all, if my salvation (or otherwise) depends simply on the will of God, why does it matter what I do? Kierkegaard therefore stresses that faith can only emerge as the final stage of life; if it is to be genuine, and not just complacency, it presupposes an understanding and an acceptance of the strenuous nature of religious demands, and their irreducibility to a merely social morality. Therefore: 'Infinite resignation is the last stage before faith, so that anyone who has not made this movement does not have faith, for only in infinite resignation do I become conscious of my eternal validity, and only then can one speak of grasping existence by virtue of faith.'[82] This illustrates well the 'dialectical' nature of Kierkegaard's thinking—infinite resignation is not the final truth, but we will not be in a position to understand the final

---

[81] B. Williams, *Morality: An Introduction to Ethics* (Cambridge, 1976), 91.
[82] *FT* 46.

truth until we have fully understood the prior positions leading up to it.

Kierkegaard describes faith as 'absurd'. Obviously, this does not mean that he considers it nonsensical or ridiculous, but, rather that it is wholly distinct from a rational, philosophical ethics. Philosophical speculation—as in Platonism—may reach the 'single-minded' position of Religiousness A, discussed at the end of the last section; it may conclude that there is a 'higher' reality, and that we should therefore, at whatever cost, will the 'one thing'—to relate ourselves to this higher world. But to believe in forgiveness and grace is possible only on the basis of faith in revelation. This is one of the central themes of the *Philosophical Fragments*, and I will discuss this and the *Postscript* in the next subsection.

4.2.2. *The Forms of 'Existential Pathos'*

We have seen in *Fear and Trembling* that a sharp distinction is drawn between religious and non-religious ethics, and also between two types of religious outlook. Kierkegaard discusses the religious life in more systematic detail in the *Postscript*, where he makes the distinction between Religiousness A and Religiousness B. 'A' is a generalized religious outlook—it involves the belief in a transcendent God, and demands of His all too human believers that they bring their wills into harmony with the divine will. No more specific theological determinations are to be brought in to complicate matters at this stage.

An obvious first answer to the question of how the religious man should live is that he should live a specifically 'religious' life; he should concentrate on striving to realize his absolute *telos*, and, as far as possible, abstract from all else. He should concentrate exclusively on a life of prayer and meditation, divorced from all worldly concerns. Kierkegaard considers this option in the course of a discussion of medieval monasticism in the *Postscript*. His attitude is sympathetic—in contrast to the bourgeois Christians of his day, at least the medievals had passion. But he still condemns monasticism as a misunderstanding.

The questionable character of the monastic movement, aside from the error of its supposed meritoriousness, lay in the fact that the absolute inwardness, presumably in order to afford an energetic demonstration of its existence, created for itself a conspicuous expression in a distinct and special outwardness. As a consequence it became, in spite of it all, only relatively different from every other outwardness.[83]

In other words, if the absolute *telos* is regarded as something to be realized by the living of a particular and distinctive way of life, it is placed on the same level as any relative *telos*. The relationship to God should be something that informs the whole of our lives, not something that is hived off as the special, full-time concern of a few lives.

So, 'The individual does not . . . divest himself of the manifold composite garment of the finite in order to clothe himself in the abstract garment of the cloister.'[84] He stays in the world. And his 'task is to exercise the absolute relationship to the absolute *telos* . . . by making the relationship to the absolute *telos* absolute, and the relationship to the relative ends relative'.[85]

What does this mean in practice? It may mean many different things in the different lives of the various individuals concerned. But, for everyone, it holds that: 'If a man shall will the Good in truth, then he must be willing to do all for the Good.'[86] Kierkegaard continues by saying 'that to will to do all is: in the commitment to will to be and to remain loyal to the Good.'[87] For the sake of his relationship to God and what flows from it, someone may have to give up all worldly goods—wealth, power, honour, admiration, love, the exercise of creative talent, freedom, life itself. Others may be able to enjoy all those things, but they can only be said to have the absolute relation to the absolute *telos* if they are prepared to renounce such things should they come into conflict with the demands of the God-relationship. The religious man does not despise worldly goods in a mood of ascetic arrogance or contempt. He wills these things, like anyone else. But he can do without them; his life is not ruined if he is deprived of them. Even the life of an 'incurable sufferer',[88] deprived of all earthly happiness, may be one of inner fulfilment, related to its absolute *telos*.

In the *Postcript* Kierkegaard outlines the various stages of religious commitment. Resignation is the 'initial expression' for the 'existential pathos' of religion. The religious man considers

---

[83] *CUP* 362–3.　　[84] Ibid. 367.　　[85] Ibid. 364–5.
[86] *P of H* 108.　　[87] Ibid. 109.　　[88] Ibid. 130–55.

how all his acts and activities can be seen in the light of his relation to God. Of all his proposed actions, he asks, not, like the Kantian: Can this action be consistently willed by me as a rational being?, but rather: Is this action compatible with retaining my relationship to God? The readiness to relinquish all is what matters.

Let the world give him everything, it is possible he will see fit to accept it. But he says 'Oh, well', and this 'Oh, well' means the absolute respect for the absolute *telos*. If the world takes everything from him, he suffers, no doubt; but he says again, 'Oh, well'—and this 'Oh, well' means the absolute respect for the absolute *telos*. Men do not exist in this fashion when they live immediately in the finite.[89]

All this, however, is only the initial expression. The 'essential expression' is suffering. We are so deeply rooted in the finite that we cannot simply cut those roots by an act of will. To come to that state of mind in which we can sacrifice all our worldly goods with an 'Oh, well', for the sake of our relationship to God, we can only suffer. For we are too committed to our temporal goods to be able to renounce them with a shrug. To relativize our worldly concerns by making the relationship to God absolute, is painful—it requires a complete existential reorientation, and this cannot be done once and for all; it needs to be constantly renewed. 'This suffering has its ground in the fact that the individual is in his immediacy absolutely committed to relative ends; its significance lies in the transposition of the relationship, the dying away from immediacy . . . self-annihilation is the essential form for the God-relationship.'[90] The religious man abandons the search for human autonomy, and admits that man *is* nothing before God and can *do* nothing before God. This uprooting of self-reliance is the suffering in the relationship to God. It is 'not flagellations and the like . . . the self-torturer does not by any means express that he can do nothing before God, for he counts his acts of self-torture as being something.'[91] In the incognito of everyday life, hiding his inner struggles from the world as carefully as the aesthete conceals himself behind his various masks, the religious man endures the purgatory of dying to immediacy.

We still have not reached the 'decisive expression' of the

[89] *CUP* 368.   [90] Ibid. 412.   [91] Ibid. 414.

religious life; this is guilt. The sermon in *Either/Or* told us that, as against God, we are always in the wrong. In our process of dying away from immediacy, there is always backsliding, wrongdoing—and therefore guilt. Maybe the wrongdoing is trivial in itself—not the sort of thing that even a sensitive ethicist like Judge William would lose sleep over—the point is that it is before God and in relation to the hope of an eternal happiness. 'The consciousness of guilt is the decisive expression for existential pathos in relation to an eternal happiness. As soon as one leaves out the eternal happiness, the consciousness of guilt also drops out essentially or it results in childish definitions which are on a par with a schoolboy's report for conduct, or it becomes a defence of civil order.'[92]

Before God, we are all guilty. For Kierkegaard, guilt is a 'qualitative', not a merely 'quantitative', concept; the fact that other people have done worse things than me, or that my failings are less now than they were before or than they might have been in the circumstances, is irrelevant. All that is relevant is that I have failed to live as I should in my relationship to God. For this, there can be no evasions, no excuses; nor can any amount of repentance wipe out the guilt. 'The eternal conservation of the recollection of guilt is the expression for existential pathos, the highest expression for it, higher than the most enthusiastic penance which would make up for the guilt.'[93] Kierkegaard argues that this should not lead to despair, for the guilt itself still indicates that we are related to an eternal happiness, to our absolute *telos*.[94] But this seems cold comfort, since the relation is a negative one; all we know is that we are estranged from our *telos*, from God, from the prospect of eternal happiness.

This is all at the level of Religiousness A, which is, to repeat, a sort of abstract model of religion in general. Much of what Kierkegaard says in this connection can in fact be seen as applying to any ethical system that postulates an absolute good or absolute *telos*. The account of 'resignation' is a conceptual analysis, drawing out the implications of what it means to believe in an overriding or absolute good. What Kierkegaard says is essentially formal or structural, and does not depend on

---

[92] Ibid. 474.   [93] Ibid. 479.   [94] Ibid. 492–3.

158   *From Ethics to Religion*

the absolute *telos* being identified in religious terms. The account
of suffering is an application of the earlier analysis to the
complexities of human psychology; given the fact of our
attachment to a variety of goods, we can only subordinate them
to the absolute through suffering. I think that this applies even
to an individual who chooses one goal as the overriding aim of
his life, without necessarily implying that it should be shared by
others (the artist who is single-mindedly devoted to his art, for
instance). Guilt is, perhaps, a different matter—the artist who
has wasted his talent may feel disgust at his failure, or even self-
hatred, but if he feels guilt this might suggest a—possibly
unconscious—sense that he had wasted a talent given by God.
Certainly, guilt as Kierkegaard describes it, as applying to
everyone, no matter how trivial his offence, would seem to be
an essentially religious concept.

Religiousness A in the *Postscript* seems to be a more
elaborately worked-out version of what Kierkegaard called
'infinite resignation' in *Fear and Trembling*. The later account is,
however, rather more pessimistic, in its stress on suffering and
guilt. In *Fear and Trembling* resignation involves pain, but the
emphasis is more on the 'peace and rest' that is purchased with
the pain.[95] For, by the act of infinite resignation, it seems that
one can attain the absolute *telos*. The finite is abandoned, but
'what I gain thereby is my eternal consciousness in blessed
harmony with my love for the eternal being.'[96] According to the
Postscript, I not only have the pain of abandoning the finite, I
also have the guilt of knowing that I am unable wholly to do so,
and therefore remain alienated from the infinite as well.
Religiousness A leaves the believer hanging between the finite
and the infinite, between earth and heaven, able neither
wholeheartedly to enjoy temporal pleasures nor to rest securely
in an assured relationship to God.

At this point, Kierkegaard brings in his account of Religiousness
B, which is actually Christianity. We might expect this to be
continuous with the attitude of 'faith' as discussed in *Fear and
Trembling*. The emphasis, however, is rather different. In the
Postscript 'B' is represented as being continuous with 'A' as far as
the element of pathos is concerned—the religious emotions or
attitudes of resignation, suffering, and guilt. But these are given

<hr />

[95] *FT* 45, 49.   [96] Ibid. 48.

a new dialectical twist by Christianity, which serves to intensify the pathos. In Religiousness A man is assumed to have within himself an essentially right consciousness of God as his absolute *telos*. Even his guilt, which cuts him off from God, remains, at the same time, a relationship to God. As Kierkegaard argued, 'truth is subjectivity'—if my attitude is one of longing for the absolute *telos*, which finds expression in resignation, suffering, and consciousness of guilt, then I am in the truth, and related to God.

This is not quite the final word, however. Kierkegaard insists that truth is subjectivity in order to turn us away from the wholly misleading attitude of objectivism. But once this has been accomplished, we may come to see that, in a still deeper sense, 'subjectivity is untruth'.[97] This is the specifically Christian viewpoint. It does not represent a return to objective philosophizing. On the contrary, it insists that, formally or ideally speaking, subjectivity is the truth—I only arrive at the relationship to God via a passionate concern to find meaning in my life, not via objective speculation. But, as a fallen creature, a sinner, wholly alienated from God, I am unable to relate to Him even through the most passionate subjectivity, for there is, from the start, a corruption, an 'untruth' within me. And 'the untruth . . . is not merely outside the truth but is polemical against the truth.'[98] I cannot extricate myself from this sorry state by my own activity, because that activity—even my deepest subjective pathos—is itself essentially corrupted. Hence, in Christianity I cease to depend on my own efforts—even in the sense of my own passive acceptance of suffering and guilt—instead, I put my faith in God not only as the *telos*, the end of my striving, that to which I must relate, but also as the one who will make the relation itself possible. According to this outlook, truth is no longer to be found within my own subjectivity, but outside me; not in any system of objective doctrine, but in Christ. Hence the difference between Christ and Socrates (Kierkegaard's paradigm of the highest kind of purely human teacher), which the *Fragments* is concerned to emphasize; Socrates is merely the occasion by which the learner is brought to realize the truth that is within him, whereas Christ brings from outside us the truth that we do not have.

[97] *CUP* 185.   [98] *PhF* 15.

As a conclusion to Kierkegaard's account of the stages of life, this seems distinctly ironical. From the perspective of what is presented as the highest stage, all the previous stages are equally distant, because in all of them my attitude to the truth remains 'polemical'. The practitioner of Religiousness A is as far removed from Christianity as the aesthete. But this is to put things rather misleadingly. Even in 'A' I fail to relate to God; but I do have the great advantage that I have reached the position from which I can make the 'leap' into Christianity. This is Kierkegaard's final understanding of the progress through the stages of life—it is a progression because it takes me from an aesthetic perspective where Christianity can only seem meaningless or nonsensical to me, to one in which it becomes a possibility for me. 'Religiousness A must first be present in the individual before there can be any question of becoming aware of the dialectic of B.'[99]

How and why does one progress from 'A' to 'B'? Why accept Christianity? Kierkegaard's answer has to do with the guilt-consciousness in 'A'. As we saw, the attempt by the individual to relate himself to his absolute *telos* did not seem to produce very encouraging results. It concludes with an attitude in which the individual is related to God 'essentially' through his suffering and 'decisively' through the very guilt that cuts him off from God. In fact, this purely natural religion, religion regarded as a human possibility rather than as divine revelation, is unable to provide us with the wholeness or fulfilment for which we were searching on the stages of life. All it can tell us in the end is that we are alienated from our *telos*, and able to relate to it only through suffering and guilt. As Karl Barth put it: 'Conflict and distress, sin and death, the devil and hell make up the reality of religion. So far from releasing men from guilt and destiny, it brings men under their sway. Religion possesses no solution of the problem of life, rather it makes of the problem a wholly insoluble enigma.'[100]

It is in this situation, when even religion—the most ambitious of human attempts to make sense of life—has broken down, that Christianity can become possible. We are told that the

---

[99] *CUP* 494.
[100] K. Barth, *The Epistle to the Romans*, trans. E. C. Hoskyns (Oxford, 1968), 258.

absolute *telos* to which we were trying, and failing, to relate has taken the initiative and related itself to us. We can then choose either to turn away in offence at such a claim, or to embrace it in faith, out of our need and our realization of the bankruptcy of all human efforts. To embrace Christianity for any other reason than the urgency of this need will, for Kierkegaard, simply mean a failure to understand Christianity, with the result that it becomes reduced to, and confused with, categories from the other stages. (Hence Kierkegaard's frequently repeated assertions that most of what passed for Christianity in the Denmark of his day was a mixture of mindless conformism, aestheticism, ethics, and Religiousness A, with speculative theological philosophizing as the icing on the cake.) Hence, it is only when someone is absolutely committed to 'his pathetic relationship to an eternal happiness', while at the same time 'his relationship to it is reduced to its minimum' because his 'guilt-consciousness is the repelling relationship and would constantly take this *telos* away from him',[101] that he will be able to accept Christianity in the right spirit.

I have suggested that Religiousness A is a development of what *Fear and Trembling* calls 'infinite resignation', and that one would therefore expect Religiousness B to be continuous with 'faith' as discussed above.[102] In Religiousness B, as in 'faith', I abandon the attempt to find fulfilment through my own efforts or even my own sufferings, and simply rely on God. To quote Barth again:[103] 'God now takes over the responsibility for us . . . our own unworthiness affects us no longer. We may now live by the fact that he does it. Which means, not a passive, but an extremely active existence.'[104] The knight of faith in *Fear and Trembling* has reached beyond the whole sphere of teleological ethics, of the inner conflict that it occasions. He does not attempt to slough off his finitude, for he knows that his

---

[101] *CUP* 497.

[102] One obvious difference is that Religiousness B is identified as Christianity, while Abraham, the paradigmatic hero of faith in *Fear and Trembling*, is a pre-Christian figure. However, for Christians, Abraham is still the 'father of faith', related in his faith to the true God.

[103] As the most sophisticated and authoritative proponent in this century of orthodox Protestant theology, Barth is a useful point of reference with which to compare Kierkegaard's views on Christianity—especially as Barth was both influenced by, and wary of, Kierkegaard.

[104] K. Barth, *Dogmatics in Outline*, trans. G. T. Thomson (London, 1982), 151.

relationship to God is not to be realized through any such heroic masochism. The emphasis in the *Postscript* is different. There it seems that the acceptance of Christianity, instead of resolving the internal divisions produced at the level of Religiousness A, simply intensifies them, makes them more painful and severe, and so heightens further the 'existential pathos' already generated by the natural religious life. Thus, in 'B', as in 'A', the individual has the task of striving in passionate inwardness to relate himself to his absolute *telos*, and thus find eternal happiness. With its insistence that we are essentially alienated from God, but can overcome this alienation by believing that God himself has taken human form and has entered the temporal world, Christianity comes along not to change the essential task of Religiousness A, but to make it harder. For in Christianity we are faced wth the absolute paradox of the Incarnation. Hence the Christian has 'to expect an eternal happiness in time through a relation to something else in time',[105] believe 'the dialectical contradiction that an eternal happiness is based upon something historical',[106] and, furthermore, 'the dialectical contradiction that the historical fact here in question is not a simple historical fact, but is constituted by that which only against its nature can become historical, hence by virtue of the absurd'.[107]

These dialectical contradictions, if believed, now increase the religious pathos for the believer—that is, they make his existence even more difficult and painful. For a start, he has to endure the 'crucifixion of the understanding'[108] which belief in these contradictions demands. Then he has to progress from guilt-consciousness to sin-consciousness. That is the realization of original sin; it is not just that I go wrong in my search for the good, or even that this wrongdoing acquires a deeper significance because it is in relation to the good; rather, I learn that I am essentially corrupted, my affinity with the eternal has been lost: 'From eternity the individual is not a sinner; so when the being who is planned on the scale of eternity comes into the world by birth, he becomes a sinner . . . existence acquires such overwhelming power that the act of coming into the world makes this being another.'[109] Thirdly, the believer faces the possibility

---

[105] *CUP* 505.   [106] Ibid. 508.   [107] Ibid. 512.
[108] Ibid. 500.   [109] Ibid. 517.

that he will lose his faith, that he will come to take offence at Christianity, and dismiss it as absurd and horrible nonsense. So indeed it is by any ordinary standard; it can only be held to by faith, which is something quite extraordinary. 'But this again is the sharpened pathos: to have constantly a possibility which if it comes to pass, is a fall just so much the deeper as faith is higher than all the religiousness of immanence.'[110] Finally, Christianity cuts its adherent off from the universally human. 'Religiousness B is discriminative, selective and polemical: only upon a definite condition do I become blessed and, as I absolutely bind myself to this condition so do I exclude every other man who does not thus bind himself.'[111] Accordingly, for the Christian, it 'may apply that he must hate father and mother. For is this not hating them as it were when he possesses his blessedness upon terms which they do not accept? And is not this a dreadful sharpening of pathos with regard to an eternal happiness?'[112]

Christianity makes other requirements as well: notably, that the individual, instead of just concentrating on his own salvation through inwardness, should perform 'works of love'. This is an important aspect of Kierkegaard's religious teaching, though it is sometimes neglected. One might ask how far it is compatible with the relativization of finite, worldly concerns. If my practical plans for helping others go wrong, can I just shrug this off with an 'Oh, well', comforting myself with the thought that my good intentions were in accord with my God-relationship? But, at any rate, this more altruistic aspect of Christian living certainly does not make it any easier. As Kierkegaard remarks, that we should be commanded to love universally is a strange thing: 'Let us consider a pagan who has not been spoiled by . . . imagining that he is a Christian—and this commandment, "Thou shalt love" will not only astonish him, but it will shock him, it will offend him.'[113] This is surely right. In Christian and post-Christian countries the strangeness of the command to love has been largely obscured by an easy sentimentality; we do not tend to think about just how radically the teaching of—say—the Sermon on the Mount contradicts the way in which we all live, or just how demanding that

---

[110] Ibid. 518.   [111] Ibid. 516.
[112] Ibid. 519.   [113] *W of L* 21.

commandment is. An 'unspoiled pagan' like Mackie is only consistent in denouncing it as 'the ethics of fantasy'.[114] For, as George Steiner says, 'By their simple presence . . . these fantastic moral requirements mock and undermine mundane values. They set anarchic love against reason, an end of time against history.'[115]

Christianity, then, is presented in the *Postscript* as the most strenuous and demanding form of human existence. To be sure, it provides consolation as well; in particular, it releases us from the unassuageable guilt associated with Religiousness A—first by proclaiming that we are not merely guilty but sinful, and then by offering the forgiveness of sins. But these consolations are bought at the price of an existence that Kierkegaard describes as 'the martyrdom of endurance'.[116] We seem far now from the serenity of the knight of faith. There is in fact, I believe, a real ambiguity in Kierkegaard's thought here. He has identified Christianity as the highest of the stages of life. Here we abandon our self-reliance, and look to God's own intervention for our salvation. But does this mean an abandonment of teleological ethics, with its striving to reach the good, or does it mean a new form of striving—a striving to reach and retain the professed salvation despite the agonizing existential pathos involved?

I do not think Kierkegaard ever really settled his own attitude to this question; and I certainly do not propose to tackle this great theological issue of faith and works, which has divided Churches and countries as well as individuals. From a philosophical point of view, I am interested in further surveying the two distinct types of religious ethics to have emerged from the discussion so far. To do so, and to round off my account of Kierkegaard's thought, the final section will look at some of the specifically religious works from his later years.

4.2.3. *Religious Ethics in Kierkegaard's Later Works*

Even considered quite abstractly and formally, the idea of an absolute *telos* raises interesting and difficult problems. I have, I

[114] J. L. Mackie, *Ethics: Inventing Right and Wrong* (Harmondsworth, 1977), 130–1.
[115] G. Steiner, *In Bluebeard's Castle: Some Notes towards the Redefinition of Culture* (London and Boston, 1978), 39.   [116] *CUP* 496.

hope, done something to indicate the appeal of this idea—if there is 'one thing' that should be the overriding object of my will, then this gives my life an overall sense of direction and purpose and provides a criterion for the ordering of my desires and ambitions, subordinating them to the overall coherence of my life. But what does this mean in practice? I have discussed the dramatic example in *Fear and Trembling* of how a commitment to the absolute may involve the sacrifice of other goods; and I have followed the more systematic discussion in the *Postscript* which produced the formula: 'an absolute commitment to the absolute *telos*, and a relative commitment to the relative ends'.[117] This remains Kierkegaard's 'official' position. But in the works following *Concluding Unscientific Postscript* he seems to waver between this and some rather different views.

Schematically, a believer in an absolute *telos* may hold any of the following views:

1. The only real good is the absolute good. In which case, one may then hold: (1*a*) that other apparent goods are actually harmful, as they tend to distract one from the absolute, and therefore should be shunned as far as possible; or (1*b*) that other apparent goods are not actually bad, but are in themselves 'indifferent'. We may take them or leave them, but in neither case are we essentially either benefited or harmed.
2. Relative goods are genuinely good, and proper objects of desire, though we must be ready to relinquish them for the sake of the absolute if necessary.
3. The absolute good is realized precisely through our enjoying a right relation to the relative goods.

This last position was the one that Kierkegaard rejected in *Fear and Trembling*; 1*a* is the ascetic or monastic attitude, which is rejected in the *Postscript*, but to which Kierkegaard becomes increasingly drawn in his later work; 2 is the position for which Kierkegaard argued in the *Postscript*, but it is easy to blur the difference between 2 and 1*b*, and Kierkegaard proceeds to do so quite frequently. The overall trajectory in Kierkegaard's later works is a movement from 2 to 1*a*, with 1*b* serving as a transitional point which helps to disguise the sharpness of the

[117] Ibid. 364–5.

move. But this progression is not at all a smooth or straightforward one, and Kierkegaard often shifts his emphasis with disconcerting abruptness within the same work.

These shifts of emphasis are clearly apparent in the *Christian Discourses* of 1848. In the section 'Joyful Notes in the Strife of Suffering' Kierkegaard's argument is that there is only one real good—the eternal—and that, therefore, if we lose worldly goods, we lose nothing of real value. 'The fact that the world bereaves thee of everything, or that thou dost lose the whole world, is really of no importance.'[118] For there is only one thing that can essentially harm us—that is sin, the state in which we cut ourselves off from the eternal by overvaluing the temporal. 'Sin is man's destruction. Only the rust of sin can consume the soul or eternally destroy it.'[119] By contrast, 'all the sufferings of the temporal are illusion', for they are not capable 'in the remotest degree of injuring the soul'.[120] So, neither temporal goods nor temporal evils really matter—they are in themselves indifferent, and only important if they distract the soul from its true good. This is what I referred to above as position 1*b*; and it is worth noting that it is not essentially Christian or even religious at all—it was a doctrine of the Stoics, of Plato at times, and even of Epicurus, who argued that the wise man could be happy even under torture. For the only true good is peace of mind, and that must not be dependent on any external circumstances.

At certain points Kierkegaard seems prepared to go even further than this, to position 1*a*, according to which worldly goods should, as far as possible, be shunned, as distractions from the true good. 'Who possesses most? Is it he who possesses God and at the same time much else, or he who being deprived of all else possesses God alone? Surely it is the latter, for all else "is loss".'[121] If one wills the absolute, then relative attachments can only hold one back; therefore 'Christianity is suspicious of marriage',[122] and suggests that one 'who wills the good [should] . . . above all things take the precaution to have no friend'.[123] There are, I think, three distinct factors underlying this radical other-worldliness, though Kierkegaard himself does not seem to distinguish them clearly. First, there is the point

---

[118] *ChD* 128.   [119] Ibid. 108.   [120] Ibid. 107.
[121] Ibid. 230.   [122] *TC* 119.   [123] Ibid. 120.

about priorities; worldly goods may not be inherently evil, but they may nevertheless serve as a distraction to one who is committed to the absolute good. Secondly, Kierkegaard becomes increasingly drawn to a dualistic outlook, according to which the temporal, the physical, and the bodily are evil; the religious task is to liberate one's immortal part, the soul, from the inherent corruption of the body. Thirdly, he takes 'worldliness' to mean sin; the world may not be inherently evil, but human nature is deeply sinful, and to act rightly is to go against the grain of that nature. It involves living as an alien in a world where social respectability is a form of compromise with sin.

During the late 1840s Kierkegaard was still not prepared to say that the only true Christian is the suffering ascetic or the martyr. Frequently, having pressed his rhetoric to what seem like extreme conclusions, he draws back again, and reverts to the old position that, in their place, relative goods are permissible or even desirable. In *The Sickness unto Death* he clearly repudiates the dualism that would identify the person with a soul imprisoned in the body. Man is a synthesis of the finite and the infinite, and to neglect either of these factors is a form of despair. Kierkegaard expressly condemns the immature religiosity that cannot be lived within the concrete circumstances of an individual's life. 'The God-relationship is an infinitising, but in fantasy this infinitising can so sweep a man off his feet that his state is simply an intoxication. To exist before God may seem unendurable to a man because he cannot come back to himself, become himself.'[124]

Even in the radical, other-worldly *Training in Christianity* Kierkegaard asserts that the chief 'moral' to be drawn from his uncompromising presentation of the demands of Christianity is simply to be honest with ourselves, to admit that we do not live up to its stringent demands. We can then, in humility, 'accept the grace which is offered to everyone who is imperfect, that is, to everyone'.[125] The person who has made this admission may then live freely and honestly—'attend to his work, be glad in it, love his wife, be glad in her, bring up his children with joyfulness, love his fellow-men, rejoice in life'.[126] What he must not do is suppose that he has fulfilled the demands of Christianity by living as a bourgeois conformist. Only by

[124] *SUD* 32.   [125] *TC* 71.   [126] Ibid.

honestly recognizing my shortcomings can I accept grace; for 'there is one sin that makes grace impossible, that is, insincerity.'[127] During the following years, however, Kierkegaard's thinking becomes harsher and more polemical, the ascetic, dualistic element comes to the fore, and he seems to repudiate the idea that we can still find grace if we honestly admit our failings. Christianity comes to mean a desperate striving to escape from this sinful world; a striving that turns life into a bitter, drawn-out agony. In the *Journals* from his last years the dominant tone is one of misanthropy, misogyny, world-weariness, hatred of the physical world, of the body, of sex, and insistence on the necessity of suffering and self-torture. 'Man is a fallen spirit . . . sent to this penitentiary, which is the world, because of his sins.' 'Christianity, and all deeper views of life . . . assume that to have dealings with the other sex spells man's degradation.' 'Christianity is the good news which turns this earthly existence into the greatest misery.' 'Spirit is to will to die, to die to the world.' 'Christianity is called, and is, hatred of man.' 'To be a Christian is the most terrible of all torments, it is—and it must be—to have one's hell on earth.'[128]

The radical dualism of Kierkegaard's later thought is a break with orthodox Christianity. Christianity is a dualistic religion, but the dualism is not of a divine, spiritual part and a finite, physical part within human nature; but a dualism of God on the one hand, and the whole of the created universe, including man, body, and soul, on the other. Asceticism, the desire of the soul to flee from the encumbrance of the body, is a natural human passion, one that has been found in the most varied cultures, including some 'Christian' ones. However, a hatred of the physical world, and the desire to escape from it, are hardly compatible with a belief in its divine creation, and must therefore appear heretical on Jewish, Christian, or Islamic standards.[129] Equally important for Kierkegaard's later thinking is his abandonment of the doctrine of salvation by divine grace. Rather, it is by our own striving that we find salvation. In the *Journals* he remarks: 'I now interpret Augustine as having hit

---

[127] ChD 195.   [128] LY 89, 93, 136, 178, 308, 347.
[129] As Michael Dummett (*Catholicism and World-Order* (London, 1979), 11) puts it: 'To aspire to be essentially other than what we are is a form of rebellion against the Creator.'

upon election by grace in order to avoid this difficulty [i.e. the strain imposed on someone by knowing that his own striving will determine his eternal destiny]; for in this case eternal salvation is not decided in relation to a striving.'[130]

He now reproaches Luther for having adopted this doctrine, and for having done so without stating clearly that it was as a concession to human weakness. In so doing, Kierkegaard asserts a radical doctrine of human autonomy. The lonely, free, responsible individual must, by his own striving, determine his destiny. Ironically, it is in this last, most polemically other-worldly, phase of his thinking that Kierkegaard comes closest to such atheistic thinkers as Nietzsche and Sartre, with their faith in the power of the individual will to impose meaning on an inherently meaningless universe. For Kierkegaard, of course, it is still towards the reality of God that the individual is striving, but it is his own will power that will determine his salvation or damnation. During the polemic against the Church establishment at the end of his life, Kierkegaard explicitly repudiated the 'moral' of *Training in Christianity*, that section quoted above which called for the individual to accept grace by humbly admitting his failures. This was no longer enough for Kierkegaard—only the unremitting struggle to find salvation would do.

This outlook did represent a new departure for Kierkegaard, for a number of his non-pseudonymous and directly religious works had expounded the doctrine of grace, bringing out clearly the difference between an ethics based on that doctrine and a teleological ethics which requires a process of striving by the individual to realize the good. I will conclude this section with some discussion of Kierkegaard's contribution to the understanding of this type of religious ethics; one that is not reducible to the structure of teleological ethics.

In *Works of Love* Kierkegaard makes an interesting distinction between an ethics of grace and one of law. In secular morality I love or feel affection for only a few particular people. For the rest of humanity I may feel a mild, generalized benevolence, but, essentially, my relations with them are regulated by notions of law, of justice, of rights. This means that I can say that someone

---

[130] *Journals* 2551.

has done me wrong, has infringed my rights, and that justice demands that restitution be made and that the offender be punished. On a religious view, I must see how my relations with other people are affected by our relations to God. But this may not essentially change the situation—I may say that God's law demands the punishment of the offender; I may appeal to God's justice to right the wrongs that have been done to me. This is, however, ruled out by Christianity. For here, in mediating my attitude to others through my relationship to God, I am forced to recognize that I am a sinner. Whatever the relative rights and wrongs of my relationships with other people, against God I am always absolutely in the wrong, infinitely indebted. God, however, forgives my sins. But, in that case, how can I have the effrontery to demand condemnation and punishment for the relative wrongdoing that someone else has committed against me? To point out the mote in someone else's eye, when God is overlooking the beam in mine? If I do so, then, Kierkegaard warns us, God will say, in effect: 'Very well. You want a legalistic, judicial attitude, rather than one of forgiveness and grace. Accordingly, I now pass judgement and condemn you.'

If, on the other hand, we accept God's grace, then this simply spills over into an attitude of love for others, one that transcends all legalism, does not stand on its rights, and forgives freely and unconditionally. I cease to think that I can gain any merit in God's eyes by my own actions or inactions, and learn to live 'solely by forgiveness'.[131] It has sometimes been suggested that this reliance on grace makes for a complacent or even amoral attitude. It was once remarked of W. H. Auden that 'To avoid despair, he has to put most of his money on Grace, since he knows he is going to fall down on Works. The trouble about such a type of Christianity is that to the outside observer it might appear to make no practical difference.'[132] Kierkegaard was very sensitive to such charges—his response in *Works of Love* was that anyone who had a genuine faith in grace would demonstrate that by his loving and non-judgemental attitude to others. Indeed, once an individual starts to judge and condemn,

---

[131] Barth, *Dogmatics in Outline*, 152.
[132] H. Carpenter, *W. H. Auden: A Biography* (Boston, 1981), 300.

he excludes himself from the sphere of grace, and puts himself back under judgement.

The man who lays hold upon the love of God, if he does not wish . . . to take it in vain [must] have an unforgettable fear and trembling, although he rests in the love of God. Such a one will certainly avoid speaking to God about another's wrong to him . . . For such a one will prefer to speak to God only about grace, in order that this fateful word 'justice' shall not cause him to forfeit everything through what he has himself evoked, the strict like for like.[133]

The cause for 'fear and trembling' here is not that I must perform the terribly strenuous task of relating to the absolute *telos* through my own efforts, but that I must constantly bear in mind that my own efforts have no merit and can achieve nothing. This attitude produces not a crushed passivity, but a freedom to live beyond the terror of the law, which 'provides simply for taking away, for imposing demands, for exhausting to the uttermost'.[134] Ethics ceases to be such an 'exhausting' process of striving towards a goal that we can never attain; it becomes a gratitude for grace which expresses itself in the love of my neighbour.

   This type of ethics still provides a criterion for the ordering of my life—of any action that I propose to take, I can ask: Is this compatible with the love of God and of my neighbour? This then forms the basis for the choice of ethical projects by which I give a specific coherence and meaning to my life. But there is no further, religious project beyond these—that of relating myself to God. It is only on the secure basis of that relation that the ethical life itself becomes possible. Hence the startling opening passage of Bonhoeffer's *Ethics*:

The knowledge of good and evil seems to be the aim of all ethical reflection. The first task of Christian ethics is to invalidate this knowledge . . . in the possibility of the knowledge of good and evil Christian ethics discerns a falling-away from the origin. Man at his origin knows only one thing: God . . . the knowledge of good and evil shows that he is no longer at one with this origin . . . He knows himself now as something apart from God, outside God, and this means that he now knows only himself and no longer knows God at all.[135]

---

[133] *W of L* 310.   [134] Ibid. 86.
[135] D. Bonhoeffer, *Ethics*, ed. E. Bethge, trans. N. H. Smith (London, 1985), 3.

By 'the knowledge of good and evil', Bonhoeffer means man's reaching for moral autonomy, the attempt either to discover or to invent for ourselves the meaning of our lives and the criterion for judging our actions. But this is destructive, for it alienates us from God, and thus from the true meaning of our lives. We are left with religion, the human effort at self-redemption, which, at its highest, produces only negation and despair. For 'man's freedom to decide . . . is not a freedom to decide between good and evil. Man is not made to be Hercules at the crossroads.'[136]

This basic outlook can still be found in the *Christian Discourses*. I have already discussed the tendency towards asceticism and renunciation to be found there. But in the first part of the book, entitled *The Anxieties of the Heathen*, Kierkegaard's argument is that it is only on the basis of one's relationship to God that one can relate properly to other goods. Their relativization is precisely what enables one to enjoy them properly, in freedom, without becoming enslaved to them. Indeed, it is the relationship to God that allows the believer to do what the aesthete had tried to do—but at the price of despair and psychological disintegration—that is, to live in the moment.

When by the help of eternity a man lives absorbed in today, he turns his back to the next day . . . one might think that the believer would be very far from the eternal when he turns his back to it and lives today, while the glimpser stands and looks towards it. And yet it is the believer who is nearest the eternal, while the apocalyptic visionary is furthest from the eternal.[137]

This is the outlook of the knight of faith in *Fear and Trembling*; he is happily absorbed in the present because his relationship to the eternal frees him from anxiety about what will happen in 'the next day'—the absolute good for him is not something that he has to obtain by struggling in time, it is given by grace. Hence, even if 'the next day' brings suffering, this does not affect what is essential in his life. The aesthete was unable to live successfully in the moment because his happiness was dependent on external circumstances.[138] 'For he whose joy is dependent

---

[136] Barth, *Dogmatics in Outline*, 56.   [137] *ChD* 76–7.

[138] This is true even of the very subtle aestheticism proposed in 'The Rotation Method' (*E/O* i. 279–96). There the aesthete is instructed on how to find amusement in even the most trivial and banal of external circumstances. But he

upon certain conditions is not joy itself, his joy is in fact dependent on conditions and is conditioned by them.'[139] But Kierkegaard goes on to define what is essentially joyful: 'What is joy? Or what is it to be joyful? It is to be present to oneself; but to be truly present to oneself is this thing of "today", that is, this thing of *being* today, of truly being today . . . Joy is the present tense, with the whole emphasis on the *present*.'[140]

This is not aestheticism, but the contrast with the ethical is most striking. Ethics is oriented to temporality, to giving a human life the unity of a narrative, to projecting a meaningful future on the basis of a sense of a meaningful past. Christian ethics, as Kierkegaard explains it here, is concerned with living in the present, living each moment in the light of eternity. The past—always a past of failure and sin—is continually being erased by the forgiveness of sins, while the future, 'the next day', is ignored. 'Take therefore no thought for the morrow: for the morrow shall take thought for the things of itself. Sufficient unto the day *is* the evil thereof.'[141] This attitude need not be thought of as abolishing ethics, but, rather, as relativizing it. Work, marriage, citizenship, still require a striving in time, the development of a narrative pattern, but they do not ultimately define me as a human individual. That, my individuality, exists prior to all social roles (though this should not be thought of as a temporal priority), being grounded in my relation to God. And this is not something that is to be understood on the model of ethical striving, something that I have to develop over the course of time; it is something that is already there in every moment, if I can only realize it. And in this realization comes the deepest immersion in existence, the fullest fulfilment of my being. 'When, by reason of silence and obedience the morrow is non-existent, today is, it *is*—and then there is joy . . .'[142]

is still dependent on having some externality which he can manipulate; left alone with his self, he despairs.

[139] *LB* 348.   [140] Ibid. 349–50.
[141] Matthew 6: 34.   [142] *LB* 349.

CONCLUSION

I have now followed Kierkegaard's account of the progress through the stages of life. In Chapter 2 I discussed—and endorsed—his polemic against objectivism. Whatever its ultimate validity, ethico-religious thinking must arise not from the dispassionate attempt to understand objectively, but from the passionate concern of the individual to find meaning in his or her own life. I hope I have shown that this does not involve a defence of arbitrariness or of the 'invention' of values by each individual—I believe that Kierkegaard shows us a way out of the sterile conflict between this subjectivism and pseudo-scientific objectivism.

In Chapter 3 I followed the argument for ethics, and concluded that there is good reason for making particular commitments and for developing the relevant virtues. But I could find no basis here for a universal morality; nor did the purely ethical sphere offer the individual any single overriding goal or *telos*. This, I argued in Chapter 4, could only be found in the religious sphere, and I followed Kierkegaard's discussion of what is involved in a commitment to an absolute *telos*, and how this attitude diverges from a pluralistic, secular morality. I hope, in this, to have refuted the claim that someone's religion cannot affect his or her ethical outlook. Nevertheless, I have argued that secular and religious morality are at least continuous, in that they seek to establish the meaning of a person's life through action directed to a goal or goals through time. But in Chapter 4 I also discussed a form of religious faith which seems more radically distinct from teleological morality. (I confined my examples to Christianity, but, as I hinted in the last section of Chapter 3, a related outlook may be found in other religious traditions.)

This work has essentially been one of criticism and clarification. I have aimed to root out some confusions and to make clearer some of what is involved in ethico-religious commitment.

Ultimately, however, it is only each individual's felt need for meaning that can determine the choices and commitments that he or she will make. Philosophy can clarify what is involved, but it cannot absolve the individual from the task of making his own decisions for himself.

BIBLIOGRAPHY

Works by Kierkegaard (arranged according to original publication date)

Either/Or (1843), vol. 1, trans. David and Lillian Swenson, with revisions by Howard Johnson, and vol. 2, trans. Walter Lowrie, with revisions by Howard Johnson (Princeton University Press, Princeton, NJ, 1971).

Johannes Climacus, or, De omnibus dubitandum est (1843), trans. Howard and Edna Hong, published with *Philosophical Fragments* (Princeton University Press, Princeton, NJ, 1985).

Fear and Trembling (1843), trans. Howard and Edna Hong, published with *Repetition* (Princeton University Press, Princeton, NJ, 1983).

Philosophical Fragments (1844), trans. Howard and Edna Hong, published with *Johannes Climacus* (Princeton University Press, Princeton, NJ, 1985).

The Concept of Anxiety (1844), trans. Reidar Thornte (Princeton University Press, Princeton, NJ, 1980).

Stages on Life's Way (1845), trans. Howard and Edna Hong (Princeton University Press, Princeton, NJ, 1988).

Concluding Unscientific Postscript (1846), trans. David Swenson and Walter Lowrie (Princeton University Press, Princeton, NJ, 1968).

Two Ages: A Literary Review (1846), trans. Howard and Edna Hong (Princeton University Press, Princeton, NJ, 1978).

Purity of Heart is to Will One Thing (1847), trans. Douglas Steere (Collins, Fontana Books, Glasgow, 1961).

Works of Love (1847), trans. David and Lillian Swenson (Oxford University Press, London, 1946).

Christian Discourses (1848), trans. Walter Lowrie (Princeton University Press, Princeton, NJ, 1971).

The Lilies of the Field and the Birds of the Air (1849), trans. Walter Lowrie, published with *Christian Discourses* (Princeton University Press, Princeton, NJ, 1971).

The Sickness unto Death (1849), trans. Howard and Edna Hong (Princeton University Press, Princeton, NJ, 1980).

Training in Christianity (1850), trans. Walter Lowrie (Oxford University Press, London and New York, 1941).

Søren Kierkegaard's Journals and Papers, ed. and trans. Howard and Edna Hong, 6 vols. (Indiana University Press, Bloomington, Ind., and London, 1967–78).

The Journals of Søren Kierkegaard, a selection ed. and trans. Alexander Dru (Oxford University Press, London and Toronto, 1940).

The Last Years: Journals, 1853–55, ed. and trans. Ronald Gregor Smith (Collins, Fontana Library of Theology and Philosophy, London, 1968).

Other Works

ADORNO, T. W., *Minima moralia*, trans. E. Jephcott (Verso, London, 1976).

ANSCOMBE, G. E. M., 'Modern Moral Philosophy', *Philosophy*, 1958.

—— *Intention*, 2nd edn. (Blackwell, Oxford, 1979).

ARMSTRONG, D. M., 'The Nature of Mind', in C. V. Borst (ed.), *The Mind/Brain Identity Theory* (Macmillan, London, 1970).

BARTH, K., *The Epistle to the Romans*, trans. E. C. Hoskyns (Oxford University Press, Oxford, 1968).

—— *Dogmatics in Outline*, trans. G. T. Thomson (SCM Press, London, 1982).

BENNETT, J., 'The Conscience of Huckleberry Finn', *Philosophy*, 1974.

BOGEN, J., 'Kierkegaard and the Teleological Suspension of the Ethical', *Inquiry*, 1962.

BONHOEFFER, D., *Ethics*, ed. E. Bethge, trans. N. H. Smith (SCM Press, London, 1985).

BORGES, J. L., 'Kafka and his Precursors', in *Labyrinths* (Penguin Books, Harmondsworth, 1985).

BRADLEY, F. H., *Ethical Studies*, 2nd edn. (Oxford University Press, Oxford, 1927).

CARPENTER, H., *W. H. Auden: A Biography* (Houghton Mifflin, Boston, 1981).

COLLINS, J., *The Mind of Kierkegaard* (Princeton University Press, Princeton, NJ, 1983).

DAVIDSON, D., *Inquiries into Truth and Interpretation* (Clarendon Press, Oxford, 1984).

DELAHUNTY, R. J., *Spinoza* (Routledge and Kegan Paul, London, 1985).

DERRIDA, J., *Of Grammatology*, trans. G. C. Spivak (Johns Hopkins University Press, Baltimore and London, 1974).

—— 'Force and Signification', in his *Writing and Difference*, trans. A. Bass (Routledge and Kegan Paul, London, 1978).

—— *Dissemination*, trans. B. Johnson (Athlone Press, London, 1981).

—— 'Signature Event Context', in his *Margins of Philosophy*, trans. A. Bass (Harvester Press, Brighton, 1982).

DONNELLY, J., 'Kierkegaard's Problem I and Problem II: An Analytic Perspective', in R. L. Perkins (ed.), *Kierkegaard's 'Fear and Trembling'*:

Critical Appraisals (University of Alabama Press, Montgomery, Ala., 1981).

DUMMETT, M., *Frege: Philosophy of Language*, 2nd edn. (Duckworth, London, 1978).

—— *Catholicism and World-Order* (Catholic Institute for International Relations, London, 1979).

EDWARDS, P., 'Kierkegaard and the "Truth" of Christianity', in P. Edwards and A. Pap (eds.), *A Modern Introduction to Philosophy* (The Free Press, Macmillan, New York, 1973).

FITZGERALD, F. SCOTT, 'The Crack-Up', in *The Crack-Up, with Other Pieces and Stories* (Penguin Books, Harmondsworth, 1983).

FOOT, P., *Virtues and Vices, and Other Essays in Moral Philosophy* (Blackwell, Oxford, 1978).

FREUD, S., *Civilisation and its Discontents*, trans. J. Strachey and W. W. Norton (New York and London, 1961).

GEACH, P. T., *The Virtues* (Cambridge University Press, Cambridge, 1977).

GEWIRTH, A., *Reason and Morality* (University of Chicago Press, Chicago and London, 1978).

GREENE, M., *Introduction to Existentialism* (Phoenix Press, Chicago, 1959).

HAMPSHIRE, S., *Morality and Conflict* (Blackwell, Oxford, 1983).

HANKINSON, J., *The Bluffer's Guide to Philosophy* (Ravette Books, Morsham, 1985).

HANNAY, A., *Kierkegaard* (Routledge and Kegan Paul, London, 1982).

HARE, R. M., *Freedom and Reason* (Oxford University Press, Oxford, 1963).

HUGHES, E. R. (ed.), *Chinese Philosophy in Classical Times* (Everyman's Library, Dent, London, 1954).

JANIK, A., and TOULMIN, S., *Wittgenstein's Vienna* (Simon and Schuster, New York, 1973).

JONAS, H., *The Gnostic Religion* (Beacon Press, Boston, 1963).

JONES, W. T., *Kant to Wittgenstein and Sartre* (Harcourt Brace, New York, 1969).

KANT, I., *Religion within the Limits of Reason Alone*, trans. T. M. Greene and H. H. Hudson (Harper Torchbooks, Harper and Row, New York, 1960).

—— *Critique of Pure Reason*, trans. N. Kemp Smith (Macmillan, London, 1982).

—— *Prolegomena to Any Future Metaphysics*, trans. P. Carus (Open Court, La Salle, Ill., n.d.).

KRIPKE, S., *Wittgenstein on Rules and Private Languages* (Blackwell, Oxford, 1982).

LOVIBOND, S., *Realism and Imagination in Ethics* (Blackwell, Oxford, 1983).

MACINTYRE, A., *After Virtue: A Study in Moral Theory* (Duckworth, London, 1981).

MACKEY, L., *Kierkegaard: A Kind of Poet* (University of Pennsylvania Press, Philadelphia, 1971).

MACKIE, J. L., *Ethics: Inventing Right and Wrong* (Penguin Books, Harmondsworth, 1977).

MARX, K., and ENGELS, F., 'Manifesto of the Communist Party', trans. S. Moore, in *The Portable Karl Marx*, ed. E. Kamenka (Penguin Books, Harmondsworth, 1983).

MURDOCH, I., *The Sovereignty of Good* (Routledge and Kegan Paul, London, 1970).

NAGEL, T., 'Subjective and Objective', in his *Mortal Questions* (Cambridge University Press, Cambridge, 1981).

NIEBUHR, H. R., *Christ and Culture* (Harper and Row, New York, 1951).

NIETZSCHE, F., *Twilight of the Idols*, trans. R. J. Hollingdale, published with *The Antichrist* (Penguin Books, Harmondsworth, 1982).

PARFIT, D., *Reasons and Persons* (Oxford University Press, Oxford, 1985).

PASCAL, B., *Pensées*, trans. A. J. Krailsheimer (Penguin Books, Harmondsworth, 1986).

PLATO, *Phaedo*, trans. R. Hackforth (Cambridge University Press, Cambridge, 1972).

PUTNAM, H., *Reason, Truth and History* (Cambridge University Press, Cambridge, 1981).

—— *Realism and Reason* (Philosophical Papers, 3; Cambridge University Press, Cambridge, 1983).

QUINE, W. V., *Word and Object* (MIT Press, Cambridge, Mass., 1960).

—— *Ontological Relativity and Other Essays* (Columbia University Press, New York, 1969).

RAMBERG, B., *Donald Davidson's Philosophy of Language* (Blackwell, Oxford, 1989).

RAWLS, J., *A Theory of Justice* (Oxford University Press, Oxford, 1986).

RICOEUR, P., *Hermeneutics and the Human Sciences*, ed. and trans. J. B. Thomson (Cambridge University Press, Cambridge, 1984).

RUSSELL, B., *The Problems of Philosophy* (Home University Library, London, 1936).

SARTRE, J.-P., *Existentialism and Humanism*, trans. P. Mairet (Methuen, London, 1948).

SCHOPENHAUER, A., *On the Basis of Morality*, trans. E. F. J. Payne (Library of Liberal Arts, Bobbs-Merrill, Indianapolis, 1965).

—— *The World as Will and Representation*, trans. E. F. J. Payne, 2 vols. (Dover Publications, New York, 1969).

SEXTUS EMPIRICUS, *Selections from the Major Writings on Scepticism, Man and God*, ed. P. Hallie (Hackett Publishing Co., Indianapolis, 1985).

STEINER, G., *In Bluebeard's Castle: Some Notes towards the Redefinition of Culture* (Faber and Faber, London and Boston, 1978).

STRAWSON, P. F., 'Social Morality and Individual Ideal', *Philosophy*, 1960.

TAYLOR, C., *Human Agency and Language* (Philosophical Papers, 1; Cambridge University Press, Cambridge, 1985).

WALKER, J., *To Will One Thing: Reflections on Kierkegaard's 'Purity of Heart'* (McGill, Queen's University Press, Montreal and London, 1972).

WILLIAMS, B., *Morality: An Introduction to Ethics* (Cambridge University Press, Cambridge, 1976).

—— 'Persons, Characters and Morality', in his *Moral Luck* (Cambridge University Press, Cambridge, 1981).

—— *Ethics and the Limits of Philosophy* (Collins, Fontana Press, London, 1985).

WITTGENSTEIN, L., *Notebooks, 1914–16*, trans. G. E. M. Anscombe (Blackwell, Oxford, 1961).

—— *Culture and Value*, trans. P. Winch (Blackwell, Oxford, 1980).

—— *Philosophical Investigations*, trans. G. E. M. Anscombe (Blackwell, Oxford, 1981).

All biblical quotations are taken from the Authorized Version.

INDEX